GLOBALISATION, HUMAN SECURITY AND SOCIAL INCLUSION

OLIVIA BOLA J- OLAJIDE ALUKO

09/02/2019
maqsur

GLOBALISATION, HUMAN SECURITY AND SOCIAL INCLUSION

OLIVIA BOLA J- OLAJIDE ALUKO

Copyright © 2018 OLIVIA BOLA J- OLAJIDE ALUKO

ISBN9781791918491

olivia4changes@gmail.com
twitter: focusbolar

DEDICATIONS

In honour and blessed memory of my late father, Professor Olajide Aluko, the first Professor of International Relations and founder of the first department of International Relations in Sub-Saharan Africa. A prolific writer on African foreign policies: Dad, your legacy lives on.

To my inspirational mother, Mrs. Ekundayo Aluko, for her support, and encouragement.

To my two sons, Isaac and Stephen, for their patience and understanding while I devoted myself to this work.

Reviews

This book is a valuable aid for those seeking to understand the African diasporic experience in the United Kingdom. By providing an in-depth account of the history of African colonisation and the subsequent push and pull factors which resulted in the movement of migrants from Africa to Britain, Olivia B. J- Olajide Aluko illustrates how the past has impacted on the lives of Africans living in Britain today. The book clarifies some of the legal issues surrounding immigrants in the UK so that those reading this volume are fully informed of the implications of being an African in Britain in the twenty-first century.

Dr Anne J Kershen FRHS FRSA
Honorary Senior Research Fellow, Centre for the Study of
Migration, Queen Mary University of London
Series Editor: Studies in Migration and Diaspora (Routledge)

This is a great book that uses research, living experience and passion to drive the reader into facts and data as it invites one to reflect deeply on the true reasons of why migrants in UK are viewed as a 'threat security challenge' instead of a contribution 'to growth', and the most 'lively expression of a global world'. With modesty and generosity, Olivia delivers a cogent analysis on why nationalist trends so often become the dominant message on the political stage rather than a multicultural resilient approach. This book presents a robust opportunity to all of us: writers; migrants; and anyone with sense of integration.

Mar. Mercedes Introini, Lawyer, Political analyst, consultant, thesustainabilityreader.com

Understanding the rationale and the historical development of African migration into the UK is essential for all scholars and politicians tackling the migration issue. Due to its clarity, depth and thoroughness, this book by Olivia B. J- Olajide Aluko is a key resource to achieving a better understanding of this huge displacement of persons.

Laura Quadarella Sanfelice di Monteforte, Director of Mediterranean Insecurity, Counter-terrorism professor at University of Rome Unicusano, Author of "Why we are under attack. Al Qaeda, the Islamic State and the do-it-yourself terrorist"

Table of Contents

Table of Figures

List of Tables

Foreword

I cannot adequately express the delight I felt when Olivia's B. Olajide Aluko invited me to write the Foreword to her latest book on 'Globalisation, Human Security and Social Inclusion'. Having read this volume, I felt all the more happy and proud at being asked to do this. No doubt, Globalisation is a notoriously difficult subject to define. Most definitions of this phenomenon have subjected it to unnatural compressions of 'time' and 'space'; however, globalisation essentially is the increasing inter-connectedness and inter-dependencies among the world's regions, nations, governments, business, institutions, communities, families and individuals. Globalisation is also a process that is geared towards fostering the advancement of a 'global mentality', and one of its most important consequences is the *deterritorialisation* of borders. What comes out quite distinctively from Olivia's B. Olajide Aluko's book is the brilliant manner in which she has used an array of sources to elucidate the links between globalisation, human security and social exclusion.

Indeed, a book like this could not have come at a better time. Some countries that have long benefitted from the contribution of others have now begun to look more 'inwards'. Britain exiting Europe and the policies of Donald Trump as American President are some recent examples of cases where former beneficiaries of a 'globalised' world have now begun to look inward when formulating their policies.

Africa has indeed made its own contributions to the world, and these have been greatly underreported. The recent wave of challenges facing the continent has sent much of its population rushing to Europe and further obscured the contributions of African immigrants to world development. What this book has shown very clearly is that Britain has benefitted from African immigrants far more than the country itself appreciates or recognises. The problematisation of Africans who have come to settle and work in Britain is fraught with ironies, which are reflected in the vocabulary of their labelling. As an unknown writer once noted, 'when people came from Europe to Africa, they were described as "Voyagers"; but when people now move from Africa to Europe they are called "Immigrants"; a group of Africans coming to Europe are labelled as "Refugees", whereas a group of Europeans coming to Africa are called "Tourists"; African People working in Europe are called "Foreigners" while European people working in Africa are called "Expatriates."' Such is the irony of migration.

It is neither historically accurate nor morally fair to see Africans and Blacks all over the world as people searching for 'freebies' and trying to reap where they have not sown. Blacks and Africans have contributed (and are still contributing) to the societies some of them now call home and it is important that this be recognised. The author has done us a great service by providing us with a detailed study that identifies and discusses the politics of migration. By arguing that migration of Blacks and Africans to Britain was sometimes encouraged and initiated by Britain, this book has genuinely broken new grounds, thus brilliantly refuting the common perception that migrations have always been self-motivated by those undertaking them. Also, by pointing out the consequences of migration on the 'haemorrhaging' countries, the book has shown the two edges of migration. Perhaps the

greatest lesson of the book is the need for tolerance and the importance of mutual appreciation. Whether we like it or not, the world has
now become so diverse and interactive that we have no choice than
to mutually reinforce the contributions of each other.

I believe that the author Ms Olivia B. Olajide Aluko has written an
extremely uplifting volume that is urbanely written and brilliantly woven together. It is a treasure of research and originality with great
depth and thoroughness, and it will put us in the author's debt for
quite some time to come.

Abiodun Alao
Professor of African Studies,
King's College London,
Strand, London

Acknowledgements

No book is just the work of one person, and this is certainly true in my case. Some of the insight, I gained in writing this volume was a combination of knowledge, secondary literature, experience, workshops, conferences, training programmes and personal dialogue with diverse groups of people.

In the preparation of this book, I have greatly benefited from the use of resources from the Questia Online Library, the National Museums Liverpool, the British Library and the Queen Mary University of London Library. Work for this book began in theory in 2009, when I completed my master's degree programme at the Queen Mary University of London. I particularly benefitted from the inputs of my past supervisors and lecturers, Prof Anne Kershen and Dr Prakash Shah. Through my exposure to their depth of knowledge, I have learned more than I could ever explain the subjects of migration, ethnicity and inclusion.

On 1 October 2016, the first edition of *Africans in the UK, Migration, Integration and Significance* was launched as a community discussion under the theme 'Globalisation, Immigration and the African diaspora'. I would like to thank everyone who was a part of the launching of the first published book.

First and foremost, I want to thank the keynote speakers who shared the enormous wealth of their knowledge during the inaugural launching of the first volume, *Africans in the UK, Migration, Integration and*

Significance. Thanks are due to Prof Abiodun Alao, Professor of African Studies at King's College, London for highlighting the contributions that have Africans have made to Britain in various academic disciplines.

Special thanks to Prof Joe Ukemenam, a Professor of Criminology and an expert on African development and confliction resolution, for his perspective on harnessing the capacity of the African diaspora in building Africa. In addition, I recognise the contributions the guest of honour on the day; African King, His Royal Highness, (HRM) Oba Dokun Thompson, the Olooni of Eti Oni, Osun state of Nigeria. HRM Oba Dokun Thompson is passionate about redefining Africa's potential and growth, especially in the area of cocoa production. It was a great privilege to have him share some invaluable insights on the cultural impacts of migration on Africa during the inaugural launch of the book 'Africans in the UK, migration, integration and significance.' Thanks to Prof Allam Ahmed, founder of Sudan Knowledge and Visiting Professor at the Royal Docks School of Business and Law and the University of Brighton. Prof Ahmed has consistently shown interest in my work and has provided me with a platform to speak alongside his experts on comparative migration issues within his network of the World Association for Sustainable Development (WASD) and Sudan Knowledge. **My gratitude also goes to other guest speakers for their insightful contributions on various topics during the inaugural book launch of 'Africans in the UK, migration, integration and significance. Thanks to Olanike Adebayo, Chinonso Ijezie, Jenny Okafor and Yemisi Jenkins MBE.**

Other people deserve recognition for contributing in diverse ways towards making this book a reality.

My profound appreciation goes to Lade Olugbemi (BA, LLB, LLM), a Housing Practitioner, Public Speaker, Human Rights Advocate, and Mental Health First Aid Trainer and the CEO of The Nous Organisation. Without her consistent motivation, which included content appraisal and feedback as well as prodding along the way, I may have deviated into another field, and the first edition of this work may likely not have advanced into a published book.

Thanks to Chris Anichie (LLB, LLM, NITA, Advocate), Resolution Accredited specialist Solicitor & Family law panellist, who encouraged me in the materialisation of my dream within the legal profession.

Special thanks to Temitope Olodo, MSC, LLB (Hons), a preventive terrorism expert, author, security strategist, and chairman of the African Security Forum UK, who suggested valuable insights into areas of national security that could impact on immigration.

I wish to thank the eldership of the Kings church ministries Chatham, for the recognition of this work, and most especially, my 'life group' family, which has been a pillar to me.

I would like to acknowledge the work of the Initiatives of Change (IOFC) UK, for the opportunity to participate in the Migrants and Refugees as Rebuilders Course (RRB) training programme, and instilling the core values of transforming lives through ethical leadership sustainable living, and trust building. To this effect, I would like to thank the RRB coordination team, Dr Muna Ismail, Peter Riddell, and Joseph Micaleff, and my other colleagues notably, Amanuel Woldesus, Joseph Ochieno, and Josephine Apira, for their keen interest in this volume,

My appreciation goes to the team at IOFC, Caux, Switzerland, notably Shontaye Abegaz, Global Coordinator of the Just Governance for Human Security, Initiatives of Change, Caux, for providing the necessary impetus for me to participate **in the Human Security X training** programme.

Although I am not a member of the Operation Black Vote UK, and the *Voice* magazine, UK, I am inspired by their work in the areas of social

justice and advancing the cause of Black minority ethnic groups in the UK. I am encouraged by the work of Migrant Voice, freemovement. org.uk and the Joint Council for the Welfare of Immigrants (JCWI) in upholding the cause of migrants and refugees in the UK. I also applaud the work of various grassroots and social justice organisations campaigning and promoting the security and safety of migrants and other vulnerable persons within our communities.

Many thanks to my siblings for been there for me, and a special thanks to my other family members for their encouragement. My heartfelt appreciation goes to all my friends, and associates, who have believed in the vision of the book, and encouraged me along the way, although I am unable to mention everyone due to space constraints. I owe a special debt of gratitude to my mother, Mrs Ekundayo Aluko, an educationist and historian, who reviewed the first edition of the book and made vital corrections that have been useful in the improvement of this new work.

I would like to thank the editorial team at University Proofreading www.universityproofreading.com) for editing the manuscript and ensuring it was ready on time for publication. Lastly, I would like to thank my publisher Sidney Sanni, for his interest in the work, and for providing useful tips on how to reach a wider audience. **I would like to acknowledge the moral support of my late uncle and family statesman, Mr Olatunji Mafolasire. Uncle 'Tunji' as he was fondly called, was looking forward to reading the book, but sadly passed on before it was completed.**

I would also like to thank the late Chief (Mrs) Modupe Aderibigbe who I would have loved to witness the completion of this edition; sadly 'mummy' as I usually call her, passed away before this book was completed.

Preface

The groundwork for this volume was laid during a presentation I gave titled 'Migration as a security threat' at the 4th Diaspora International Conference organised by the World Association of Sustainable development(WASD) in the UK. Thus, this work is a contribution to a large body of literature on migration studies throughout the whole world.

The process of writing this book has come at a time when a spotlight has been placed on immigration as a growing danger to national security. In the past decade, influxes of migrants into the UK have generated new challenges of balancing national security with human security for nation states, as a consequence of which apathy and antipathy towards newcomers is becoming a widespread issue, with many international communities slamming their doors on further immigration.

It is indisputable that many of the world's developed nations, including the USA, Canada and the UK, were built through the influxes and contributions of immigrants. Throughout Britain's history, immigrants have played a vital role in the nation's cultural, economic and political development, and many quintessentially 'British' elements in fact derive from her non-native populations. Even the popular fish and chips dish that is regularly enjoyed by and widely considered as emblematic of modern British cuisine was introduced by Western Sephardic Jews who settled in England in the 17th and 18th centuries, and the first fish and chips shop was opened in 1860 by Joseph Malin, a Jewish immigrant from Eastern Europe (Rayner, 2005).

The term 'migration' is often conflated with the similar phenomenon of 'immigration'. In simple terms, migration denotes the act of moving from one place to another, whether within a country or across borders. Such movement can represent a momentary or seasonal spatial shift at the individual or family levels, or it can involve a larger scale displacement affecting larger groups or even whole communities, which might be more permanent. Immigration, on the other hand, is described as the movement of non-natives into a country based on the desire for better living conditions and places to settle. This kind of movement is usually controlled by the destination countries, which can choose to either admit or to exclude incomers through the mechanisms of immigration policy.

The movement of people to other countries has been a phenomenon throughout the history of the human race; however, the nature of migration has experienced a profound shift in more recent years. The International Migration Report 2017 reported that approximately 258 million people now live in places outside their countries of birth, which equates to about 3.2% of the world population (United Nations, 2018). Factors such as conflict, poverty, human rights abuses, national security, human security and a host of other problems are the principal drivers of migration. Globalisation has made it more possible than ever before for people to move from one country to another, whether permanently or over the short-term. With the ease of transportation and improved communication- and information- sharing through different online platforms, people are more aware of the opportunities that exist in other countries.

Globalisation has opened avenues for goods and services to be exchanged between countries, thus increasing the tradability of skills and services-oriented activities. With increasing opportunities for jobs in certain sectors in the UK, it has sometimes been relatively easy for migrants to enter and work in the UK, as they have helped fill shortages in many areas of need, such as in the National Health Service (NHS). However, this situation has created new challenges for international communities, as countries struggle to balance economic growth with unease over outsiders. The expansion in commerce driven by globalisation has greatly benefitted the UK economy; however, recent issues associated with Brexit have caused uncertainties concerning the future of trade, and one will not know to what extent that this process fully impacts the economy until after the deals with the European Union (EU) are concluded.

The Brexit vote was largely driven by the British public's fears about mass immigration from Europe, and one of the major reasons for the European Union (EU) referendum of 23 June 2016 was to 'reclaim' British borders. Voters hope that Brexit will curtail free movement from the EU, which the government has said is on sustainable levels. An abiding concern has been that standards of living might fall due to rising challenges to British natives in the labour market if the mass population of migrants and refugees are allowed into the UK. Thus, many have deduced that the primary reason why 17.4 million Britons voted to leave the EU was to reduce immigration and its perceived threat to social and economic structures here in the UK. Others have argued that the real problems of immigration originate not with the EU migrants, but rather with those from outside the Eurozone. Approximately 184,000 migrants arrived in the UK from the EU in 2015, whereas some 188,000 migrants entered from non-EU countries over the same period (Arnheim, 2017).

Aside from the challenges posed by economic migrants, the UK is also faced with the obligation of balancing its responsibilities to asylum seekers as part of its international legal obligations. In fulfilling these duties, the British asylum system has remained complex in a manner that is viewed by many as inhumane. Whereas a few refugees—such as many applicants from Eritrea and Iran—have been granted asylum in the UK, others have been refused at high rates (Table 1, Figure 1; British Refugee Council, 2017). Of the tens of thousands of asylum applications made in the year leading up to June 2017, only 34% of seekers were granted protection, while the remainder were told it was perfectly safe for them to return to the areas that they were fleeing. Reports also show that 80% of UK councils have failed to take in *any* refugees since 2015, thus leaving many homeless and/or resorting to begging in order to feed themselves and their children. Much like in the 1950s and 1960s, the public has used immigration as bait to canvass for those political figures whose policies disfavour immigration. Subsequently, new immigration policies have been introduced to make it more difficult for people from outside the European Union to come to the UK, and more recently, the status of EU members after Brexit is also being discussed.

UK asylum applications

Applications for refugee status or another form of international protection in the United Kingdom, including dependants

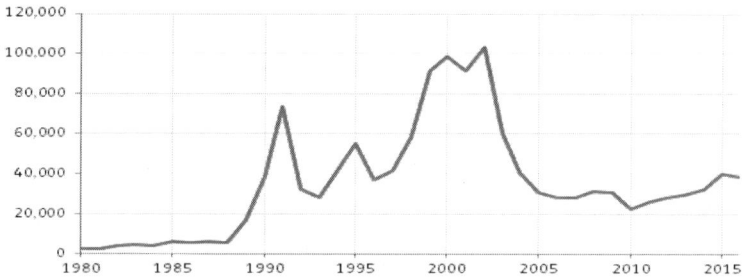

Source: Home Office, "Immigration Statistics, October to December 2016", asylum data tables, volume 1, table as_02.

Figure 1. UK asylum and protection applications, 1980-2015[1]

Table 1.[2] Asylum decisions by nationality, Q 3 2017: Top ten countries for number of decisions

Country	Decisions	Refugee status	Humanitarian protection	Discretionary Leave	Other grants	Refusals
Iran	627	313	10	0	17	296
Pakistan	496	71	0	3	3	419
Iraq	466	64	12	1	41	348
Bangladesh	363	12	0	2	0	349
Afghanistan	277	86	1	1	27	162
Eritrea	244	202	0	0	2	40
India	232	0	0	4	0	228
Sudan	223	94	0	0	3	126
Nigeria	219	19	0	2	8	190
Sri Lanka	169	11	0	0	1	157

[1] Source: Home office, 'Immigration Statistics, October to December 2016', asylum data tables, volume 1, table as_02

[2] Source:https://www.refugeecouncil.org.uk/assets/0004/2379/Asylum_Statistics_Nov_2017.pdf

As shown in Figure 2, most migrants who have arrived in the UK came to study, whereas others came in search of work. According to a report compiled by the Migration Advisory Committee (MAC), although most immigrants from the EU have little-to-no impact on employment of UK-born workers, entrants from non-EU countries have more influence across the public and private sectors, and the probability of a negative impact on natives is greater during economic downturns. The MAC distinguished between two sub-periods in its analysis of the specific impacts of EU and non-EU migrants: 1975-1994 and 1995-2010; finding that non-EU immigration was associated with a reduction in the employment of UK-born workers during the latter period (Migration Advisory Committee, 2012). Entrants from countries that are not members of the EU are subject to the strict immigration controls that were introduced in July 2012.

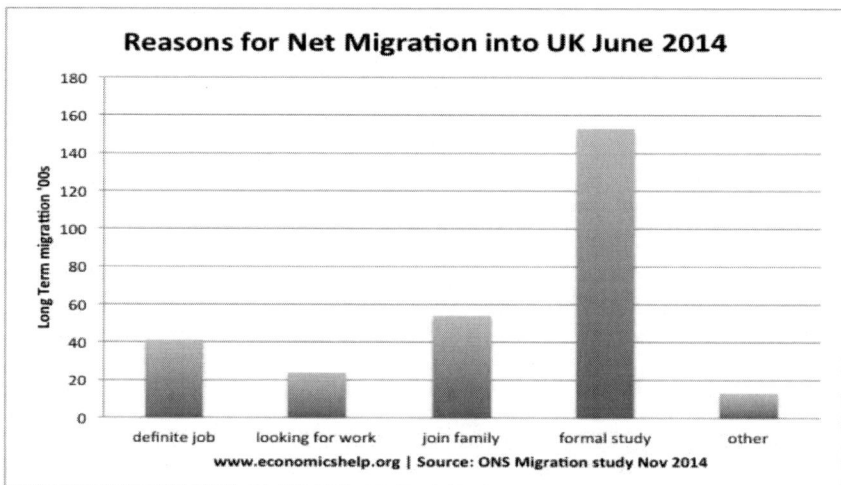

Figure 2.[3] Reasons for Migration to the UK, June 2014

[3] Source: Migration Statistics Quarterly Report: November 2014.
Office for National Statistics. Retrieved from https://www.ons.gov.uk/
peoplepopulationandcommunity/populationandmigration/internationalmigration/

National Security vs. Human Security

Why has a nation that once favoured migration and celebrated its ethnic diversity introduced such stringent immigration controls to the extent that it has impacted the opportunities available to vulnerable migrants and refugees? Perhaps the new British immigration policy may be understood within the context of globalisation and national security concerns. Concerns over terrorism figure prominently among the reasons why many Western governments have introduced immigration restrictions, though there are other, unrelated economic and social concerns that cannot be wished away. Post 9/11 issues of security have loomed large in immigration debates, which are stimulated by the panic over immigrants' dominating the labour market and the demand for more stringent policies to obstruct foreign-born terrorist infiltration from abroad (Hauptman, 2013). A few years after the 9/11 attacks, suicide bombers killed about 56 people in the UK on 7 July 2005, and another suicide bomb attack was foiled on 25 July 2005. Thus, new terrorism laws were introduced in the UK to safeguard against such events in the future. Nonetheless, there has been a steady increase in terrorism, particularly in Europe and UK, which have severely impacted upon British society. According to the Global Terrorism Database, approximately 126 people were killed in the UK by terrorist attacks between 2000 and 2017 (Kirk, 2017). The awareness of unpredictable violence negatively impacts daily life, as one cannot adequately prepare for it, and among many, the

---

bulletins/migrationstatisticsquarterlyreport/2015-06-30

fear is so compelling that 'every Muslim became a person of sus-picion' (Simpson, 2017).

Demographic changes in the UK are also among the reasons giv-en for the tightening of the UK's security borders. Critics of immi-gration have asserted that amidst a myriad of problems caused by the bid to promote a multicultural Britain, the influence of immigrants has altered the meaning of 'Britishness'. Table 2 illus-trates the percentage of people from various nations who came to the UK in 2015, with Nigeria and South Africa being the major sending countries. Table 3 shows that of the 322,000 non-British people who have immigrated to the UK in 2018, nearly 73% are from non-EU countries. Approximately a third of people currently living in the UK are immigrants, and there is a concern that these numbers may increase to unimaginable levels if controls are not exercised, particularly against migrants and refugees from the Middle East and Africa ('People must open eyes to new reality': Experts to RT in wake of Barcelona carnage', 2017). The influx of migrants between 1997 and 2010, which was facilitated by the then Labour Party government, has changed the racial composi-tion of Britain; new demographic estimates suggest that a third of the UK population will be Black or from another ethnic minor-ity by 2030 (Lyons, 2014), and it is feared that white Britons will be in the minority by 2066 if immigration continues at the same rate (Silverman, 2013). This could be one of the reasons why im-migration rules are being tightened for entrants from non-EU countries.

Table 2.[4] Top ten sender countries of migrants by country of birth and nationality, UK 2015

Country of birth	Percentage share	Country of citizenship	Percentage share
India	9.0	Poland	15.7
Poland	9.5	India	6,4
Pakistan	5,9	Ireland	6.2
Ireland	6.0	Italy	3.7
Germany	3.3	Pakistan	3.2
South Africa	2.2	Romania	3.5
Nigeria	2.3	Lithuania	3.3
Bangladesh	2.3	Portugal	4.1
Romania	4.0	France	3.1
Spain	2.8	Germany	2.7

Table 3. Latest UK migration statistics, year ending March 2018

	All Citizenships	British	Non-British	EU	Non-EU
Immigration	614,000	72,000	542,000	226,000	316,000
Emigration	344,000	124,000	219,000	138,000	81,000
Net Migration	271,000	-52,000	323,000	87,000	235,000

Prejudice towards immigrants is often expressed in statements by the media, politicians and the public at large, such as 'foreigners are taking jobs British people could do', or 'immigrants come to the country and consume the wealth of the country without having created anything'. The UK workforce comprises about 31.6 million people, of which 5.4 million are non-native born workers (Chu, 2016). Nonetheless, immi-

[4] Adapted from 'Migrants in the UK: An Overview'. By C. Vargas-Silva & C. Rienzo (2017, 21 February). Retrieved from http://www.migrationobservatory.ox.ac.uk/resources/briefings/migrants-in-the-uk-an-overview/.

grants still comprise only a small fraction of the UK population, and there is evidence that they contribute more to the economy than they detract. According to a *Guardian* report from 2013, migrants contribute over £25bn to the UK economy, and residents from the European Economic Area countries have paid 34% more in taxes than they received in benefits. ('Migrants Contribute £25bn to UK Economy, Study Finds', 2013). Figure 3 depicts the contributions made by different streams of immigrants, which contradict biased claims that immigrants come to the UK to live off public services.

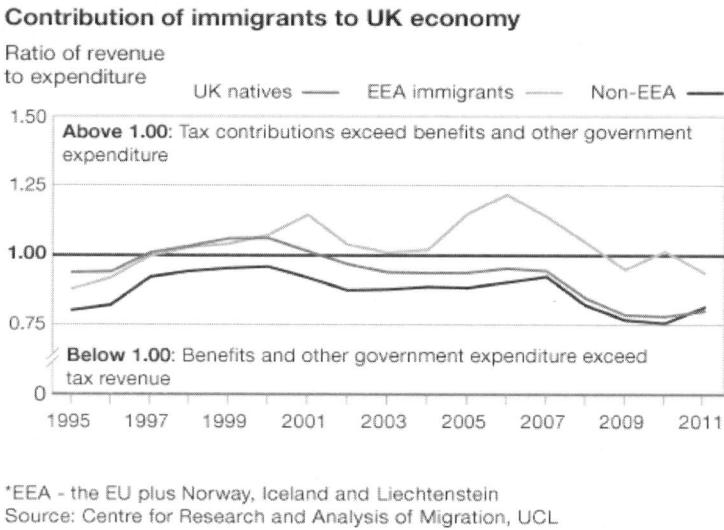

Contribution of immigrants to UK economy

Ratio of revenue to expenditure

UK natives ——   EEA immigrants ——   Non-EEA ——

Above 1.00: Tax contributions exceed benefits and other government expenditure

Below 1.00: Benefits and other government expenditure exceed tax revenue

*EEA - the EU plus Norway, Iceland and Liechtenstein
Source: Centre for Research and Analysis of Migration, UCL

Figure 3. Contribution of immigrants to the UK economy

Although many European countries have continued to restrict the number of refugees allowed to cross into their borders, the United Nations reported that African nations have taken in about 80% of the world's refugees (Momodu, 2016/2017), 740,000 of whom have been hosted by Ethiopia alone. These refugees are from Eritrea, Somalia, Sudan and South Sudan. This is hardly publicised, leaving the world with the false impression that those fleeing conflict are all headed to Europe. The activities of Boko Haram in the Northern Part of Nigeria have caused two million people to be forcibly displaced, and about 195,350 people have since sought refuge in neighbouring countries in Africa like Cameroon, Chad and Niger (Momodu, 2016/2017). This indicates that alternatives closer to home exist for those refugees who become entangled in policies reinforcing that they are unwelcome in the UK.

Immigration opponents have long argued that immigrants do not integrate into British society, but rather live parallel lives. Opponents of immigration reform have supported new controls and argue that immigrants from other cultures are destroying 'Britishness'. If integration constitutes assimilation into British values, and there are a host of variables of integration, how can it be measured? Different factors influence whether migrants assimilate the culture of the British society or remain ensconced within the comforts of their own cultures, and age at the time of migration, place of birth and ancestry all operate to influence an individual's integration process.

This volume examines the history of Black immigration in the UK from the perspectives of those who arrived in this country in search of better lives, as well as those who have felt threatened by the impact of Black immigration on their own economic positions and social identities. It is important to note that although immigration has come to be considered a major global threat, there are other significant issues threatening global and regional stability, such as food, health, economic, environmental, personal, community and political security, which are the seven categories of human security identified by the United Nations Development Report (UNDP, 1994). This work particularly seeks to balance imperatives of national security, which has become increasingly tenuous as borders become more malleable and vulnerable, with concerns of human security, as sought by migrants fleeing untenable conditions in their homelands. It is hoped that those who read this study will come away with a more informed understanding of both priorities.

References

Alibhai-Brown, Y. (2015, 12 July). White people may deny it, but racism is back in Britain. *The Independent*. Retrieved from http://www.independent.co.uk/voices/comment/white-people-may-deny-it-but-racism-is-back-in-britain-10384129.html

Arnheim, M. (2017, 07 February). The Non-EU migration problem that can't be fixed by Brexit - But which could have been solved years ago. *The Huffington Post*. Retrieved from http://www.huffingtonpost.co.uk/dr-michael-arnheim/eu-migration_b_10776806.html

British Refugee Council (2017). Quarterly asylum statistics, November 2017. Stratford, UK. Retrieved from https://www.refugeecouncil.org.uk/assets/0004/2379/Asylum_Statistics_Nov_2017.pdf

Chu, B. (2016, 05 October). What do immigrants do for the UK economy? Nine charts Conservative ministers seem to be ignoring. *The Independent*. Retrieved from http://www.independent.co.uk/news/business/news/immigration-uk-economy-what-are-the-benefits-stats-theresa-may-amber-rudd-tory-conference-speeches-a7346121.html

Hauptman, S. (2013). *The criminalization of immigration: The Post 9/11/Moral Panic* (The new Americans: recent immigration and American society). El Paso, TX: LFB Scholarly Publishing.

Kirk, A. (2017, 17 October). How many people are killed by terrorist attacks in the UK? *The Telegraph*. Retrieved from http://www.telegraph.co.uk/news/0/many-people-killed-terrorist-attacks-uk/

Lyons, J. (2014, 06 May). Up to 'a third of UK population will be black or from another ethnic minority' by 2050. *The Daily Mirror*. Retrieved from https://www.mirror.co.uk/news/uk-news/up-a-third-uk-population-3500561

'Migrants contribute £25bn to UK economy, study finds'. (2013, 05 November). *The Guardian*. Retrieved from https://www.theguardian.com/uk-news/2013/nov/05/migration-target-useless-experts

Migration Advisory Committee. (2012). Analysis of the impacts of migration. Retrieved from https://www.gov.uk/government/uploads/system/uploads/attachment_data/file/257235/analysis-of-the-impacts.pdf

Momodu, S. (2016 December – 2017 March). Africa most affected by refugee crisis: Ethiopia and Uganda praised for open-door policy. United Nations Africa Renewal. Retrieved from https://www.un.org/africarenewal/magazine/december-2016-march-2017/africa-most-affected-refugee-crisis

OECD & UNDESA (2013). World migration in figures. Retrieved from https://www.oecd.org/els/mig/World-Migration-in-Figures.pdf

'People must open eyes to new reality': Experts to RT in wake of Barcelona carnage. (2017, 18 August). Retrieved from https://www.rt.com/news/400053-barcelona-terrorism-new-reality/

Rayner, Jay (2003, 19 January). Enduring Love. *The Guardian*. Retrieved from https://www.theguardian.com/lifeandstyle/2003/jan/19/foodanddrink.restaurants

Silverman, R. (2013, 02 May). White Britons 'will be minority' by 2066, says professor. *The Telegraph*. Retrieved from http://www.telegraph.co.uk/news/uknews/immigration/10032296/White-Britons-will-be-minority-by-2066-says-professor.html

Simpson, F. (2017, 30 December). 'Every Muslim became a person of suspicion' after UK terror attacks, woman trolled for wearing a hijab says'. *The Evening Standard*. Retrieved from https://www.standard.co.uk/news/uk/every-muslim-became-a-person-of-suspicion-after-uk-terror-attacks-woman-trolled-for-wearing-a-hijab-a3728871.htmlhttps://www.standard.co.uk/news/uk/every-muslim-became-a-person-of-suspicion-after-uk-terror-attacks-woman-trolled-for-wearing-a-hijab-a3728871.html

United Nations. (2017). International migration report, 2017. Retrieved fromhttp://www.un.org/en/development/desa/population/migration/publications/migrationreport/docs/MigrationReport2017_Highlights.pdf

United Nations Development Programme (UNDP) (1994). Human Development Report 1994: New Dimensions of Human Security. Retrieved from http://hdr.undp.org/en/content/human-development-report-1994

Introduction

This volume will begin by considering the subject of the Black presence in Britain and touch on other social and historical issues that impact upon their migration generally.

The term 'Black people' refers to a human group whose skin colour are perceived to be dark-skinned, as well as an identity for black people of African origin and South Asia. In the UK, 'black' is used as a terminology to describe people who are of non-white descent. This description, which is considered derogatory, has undergone various changes since the 1950s. By the 1990s, it was no longer considered correct to describe people by their race; rather, it has become more acceptable to describe people according to their ethnicity. The Office of National Statistics (Gardener & Connolly, 2005) adopted Bulmer's (1996, p.35) definition of an ethnic minority group as a collective group within a wider population 'having real or putative common ancestry, memories of a shared past, and a cultural focus upon one or more symbolic elements which define the group's identity, such as kinship, religion, language, shared territory, nationality or physical appearance'. For example, in 1991, a change in the census form meant that people were requested to declare their ethnic group rather than their 'race'. By the 2001 census, people were formally classified according to a system that created various ethnic groups, which impacted upon the way White, Asian,

Mixed, Chinese, Black and other groups were classified. Thus, those who identified their race as 'White' could choose an ethnic identity as 'White British' or as 'White other', whereas those identified as 'Black' had the option of identifying either as 'Black African' or 'Black Caribbean'. By 2011, the ethnic classifications had become more diverse, as it became more acceptable to define Black people as BME (Black and Minority Ethnic) or BAME (Black, Asian, and Minority Ethnic). The BME classification is now used to describe peoe ple from Africa, Caribbean and their descendants who may be third or fourth generation Black British. The terms 'immigrant', 'refugee', and 'migrant' are used to denote those who came from other lands to live permanently in the UK, which includes groups classified as BME and BAME. When immigration policies are either relaxed or tightened, it is these BME/BAME immigrant ethnic groups that benefit or are placed at a disadvantage.

There is a widespread concern that the migrant and refugee crisis within Europe can no longer be managed and might spiral into the UK if not curtailed. Media messages of the African immigrant and refugee 'crises' continue to fill many newspaper pages and dominate political debate. It is especially feared that these migrants—including refugees from Syria and other developing countries, as well as an estimated one million economic migrants and conflict refugees from Libya and sub-Saharan Africa driven by a search for safety and job opportunities (Wintour, 2017)—will ultimately find their way to Europe and eventually enter the UK through other, unofficial border routes.

No doubt, Britain has closed the door on immigration; however, some communities have been more visibly affected by these closures than others. Some within the African and Caribbean community have been adversely impacted by the changes to immigration policies that came into effect in July 2012, particularly the new restrictions on family migration, and the Tier 2 permit system has thrown many a genuine immigrant off-balance.

History has shown that governments have often pandered to the cries of the public over immigration, and this has proved true over the last decade. Recent poll findings have demonstrated a specific desire by the public to reduce immigration from Africa. A survey gauging the feelings of the British populace about immigrants demonstrated that a majority of White British currently seek a reduction in immigration rates, even at the risk of declining skill levels on the jobs market (Kaufman, 2018). Whereas respondents indicated that highly skilled immigrants remained welcome, the approval numbers were sharply reduced when considering people from Africa and Asia (Kaufmann, 2018). Such reports indicate that Africans might be perceived as a security threat. If this is the case, could it be that the presence of Africans in the UK is a cause for concern due to a renewed or sudden appearance, or are current sentiments merely a continuation of ongoing negative perceptions of 'Black people'?

One way to address this question is to consider the position of 'Black people' in the history of immigration to Britain. Between 1045 and 1945, various streams of immigrants, ranging from the Dutch to Germans, Jews, Huguenots, Irish, Asians, Caribbeans, and Africans all came to settle in Britain. Although all of these immigrants faced challenges in their attempt to settle in the UK and assimilate within British society, a great deal of evidence indicates that a more deeply entrenched intolerance for Africans has existed since the Transatlantic slave trade, when Black African captives were sold and shipped into Britain and treated with disdain by their masters as well as the wider society. The forced migration of Black slaves from Africa to Britain marked a turning point for Britain's White community, as will be discussed in Chapter 2. Later, as discussed in Chapter 3, more voluntary forms of migration occurred during the British colonial period, as many middle-upper class Africans and Caribbeans came to Britain through the interconnected colonial education system to study at various universities. After World War II, larger influxes began to arrive as Britain recruited Blacks and Asians to rebuild the country, and more students and workers began arriving over the next twenty years as opportunities opened to them with the ending of British colonial control. These people might have 'belonged' to the British Empire (later the Commonwealth) by right of nationality; however, they were treated as foreigners and second-class residents by many of the White native British, who saw them as a threat to their jobs and economic security, and numerous attacks were levelled against members of ethnic minority groups in expressions of discrimination and hostility. Nonetheless, they continued to arrive and take jobs as manual workers, cleaners, drivers and nurses, building small diaspora enclave communities that provided some shelter from conflict with natives, taking whatever jobs were offered, yet also producing children who became 'truly' British despite their segregated lives, attending British schools and developing a new identity as Black Britons, and striving for recognition and equality in UK society.

Enormous racism and discrimination were experienced by the Black Caribbeans who migrated to the UK from the mid-1940s to 1960s. Despite these unpleasant historical experiences, it can be stated that there have been numerous improvements in racial equality since the first Race Relations Act was enacted in Parliament in 1965. The aim of this act was to address racial discrimination by making it unlawful to discriminate against other people on the grounds of their race, colour, or national origins in public places. Subsequent Acts have been introduced and implemented since then, including the Equality Act 2010, which provided legal protections from discrimination in the workplace as well as wider society. Over the years since the 19th century, when most BME were not allowed to own anything and free labourers had limited opportunities for job advancement, there have been significant improvements in the employment outcomes of BME people in the UK, and in the political arena, the UK has experienced an increase in the number of Black and Minority Ethnic MPs and counsellors, particularly within the Labour Party. Moreover, as noted above, in more recent decades, we have seen BME people in the UK described not only by reference to race, but also by ethnicity, as the term 'Black Minority and Ethnic' has come into use to describe people of African- and Caribbean heritage.

However, anti-immigrant sentiments have not changed greatly in the 21st century, and racism remains endemic in UK society. Although direct forms of racism are denounced, and ordinarily, people may not be discriminated upon based on their race, racism still abounds in subtle but institutionalised forms that are more difficult to prove. In the words of 'Brown 'though there may indeed be 'much national outrage when well-known people use words that are deemed offensive' (Alibhai-Brown, 2015), there is less concern shown in the face of other exercises in discrimination, prejudice, violence and common bigotry. Threat perceptions about immigrants have often underlain the immigration policies that target and exclude Black and Minority Ethnic groups.

The term 'institutionalised racism' should not be used carelessly without an understanding of its meaning, which can be partly achieved by considering some examples. Institutional racism is often subtle and is not usually noticed except through investigation, probing, and statistics. This includes organisational structures and the diversity of people in leadership positions, notwithstanding that a lot of organisations may pride themselves for having demographically variable personnel. Evidence of racism might also include the disproportionate awards and acclamations that are credited to 'white' people in academics, sports, music and acting. Moreover, there is still more work that needs to be done to create equal opportunities for Black and Minority Ethnic (BME) population in the labour market. For example, people of colour often experience limited labour mobility, as subtle glass ceilings keep certain members of the BME groups from achieving their career potential. There is evidence that many Black, Asian and minority ethnic people still face a significant jobs gap and pay penalty despite the increasing numbers of members of these groups who are obtaining advanced degrees (Slawson, 2017). There seems to be a deliberate failure to acknowledge the multifaceted contributions of the non-White communities in the UK.

Nevertheless, many Black people remain proud to identify themselves as members of British society, and those who have naturalised as citizens are often particularly prone to tout their status. Having known no other society, Black Britons more commonly identify themselves as 'British', and some may even tick 'Black British' instead of 'Black African' on their ethnicity questionnaire. However, in common, everyday interactions with British natives, some people of African descent have reported that even though they see themselves as 'British', other British natives regularly inquire about their origins, and their identification with British nationality is met with the response, 'yes I know', which is immediately followed by 'where are you originally from?' Such incidents remind them that even while they might be included in British society by right of nationality, in reality, their visible ancestral roots continue to define them as 'immigrants'. This is not necessarily always a negative reaction or summation of the questioners; however, it does show that being British by birth does not necessarily make you 'English', but rather only guarantees that you have national status as a part of your civil rights. During my interviews with British natives in the suburbs, I noted that many views expressed about immigrants were based on false perceptions and misinformation received from the media. For example, as one of the people I interviewed complained, 'I go to work just like any other person. Immigrants should go to work and not come to the country to claim benefits. Another interviewee expressed resentment that unlike those born in the country, immigrants 'do not pay tax'. Overall, 30% of the people engaged in random interviews felt that immigrants mainly came to the UK to apply for public benefits.

Although British society ostensibly strives to tolerate people of other cultures and allow them to flourish within their chosen diasporas, the kind of respect that is accorded to white Britons who visit or settle in Africa is not reciprocated in the UK. Some of the most negative perceptions held by the public are found among British natives who have not visited Africa or engaged with Africans in the community. White visitors to Africa have been known to be treated with utmost respect and even preferential treatment; however, it is doubtful whether any Black African can boast of such reciprocal treatment on English soil. On the other hand, I have observed that many British natives who have worked and lived in Africa show a different level of respect for

Black Africans when they meet them in the UK, and one common claim they have made is that the Africans were very creative, generous, kind and hospitable towards them. However, historically Black African migrants to the UK have been alternately identified as victims or villains, and those who are celebrated as heroes are usually dead by the time that praises are poured upon them during Black History Month.

Immigration is often viewed based more on population estimates and rarely by the contributions of migrants to the economy. Some members of the public perceive immigration as a problem based on the number of ethnic minorities, they see around them, particularly in larger cities like London, where new migrants have been depicted as 'cockroaches' (Alibhai-Brown, 2015). However, all ethnic minorities living in the country are not immigrants, and visible appearance or accents are not sufficient to identify who is an 'undocumented 'versus 'legal' immigrant, nor can merely observing the physical characteristics of passengers at a train station provide evidence for undocumented immigration, as many or all the Black passengers observed may well be Black British who have no direct links to any other country. What classification would an opponent of immigration apply to these categories of individuals?

'Black African' ethnicity cannot be compartmentalised into one stream, as the political, economic and social makeup of their backgrounds of Africans is varied. For example, the experiences of 'African boat migrants' who entered the UK after voyaging across the Mediterranean Sea are quite distinct from migrants who made a decision to apply for a visa and arrived at the UK legally. It is typical for many Nigerians or Ghanaians to voluntarily decide to come to the UK and retain thriving family support networks; however, the same cannot be said of those Africans who have been forced to flee their countries due to conflicts or famines, such as the Calais migrants currently stationed in various refugee camps; their experience is quite different from other refugees who came here legally to seek asylum. It is doubtful if such differences are recognised by the British public, for whom it remains difficult to distinguish a Black African migrant who is in the UK legally from an 'undocumented immigrant'. Moreover, as noted at the beginning of this introduction, the term 'Black' is widely used to describe many people who are of non-white descent or whose colour is perceived to be dark-skinned, even though not all Black people are Africans, and not all Black people identify themselves as 'Africans'. One should not assume that because an individual 'is dark skinned' that he or she is from Africa, because many people who are dark skinned and referred to as 'Black people' have their roots and ancestry in other places, such as South Asia, the Americas, New Zealand, or Australia. One might ask who are the people that can be classified as 'Africans', and under what criteria are they so categorised? Africans themselves rarely identify themselves by 'race', but rather tend to define themselves as members of states, religions and ethnic groups; 'Black' only becomes a social construct once Black Africans are in a country where they are a visible minority. Professor Ali Mazrui has distinguished between 'Africans of the blood' and 'Africans of the soil', whereby while the former is defined by race and genealogy, and the latter is identified by geography and ancestral location (Mazrui, 2009). Some people who are of 'African descent' see themselves as 'Black British', rather than as part of an African diaspora, and may struggle to identify with their African roots. Though they might be Africans by heritage or even birth, upon becoming British nationals they choose to identify themselves by the nationality of their residence.

People in this category have chosen to assimilate into the British way of life, imbibing local mannerisms and culture and cutting off any social links to their heritage.

Although people from Africa are classified as one ethnic group under the UK census statistics, the Black African group is highly diverse, and this ethnic classification is not sufficient to capture all of these distinctions. Aside from the regional differences that exist between North Africa, South Africa, and East and West Africa, there are many variations in economic, political and social status within and between these societies, and issues such as religion and cultural diversity must also be taken into consideration. Minority ethnic groups are differentiated based on a combination of categories that include 'race', or skin colour, national- and regional origins and language. For instance, people from Nigeria, Sierra Leone, Kenya, Gambia, Uganda, Sudan, Somalia and Ghana all have individual and cultural differences based on diverse languages, values and origins. These issues influence the drivers of migration, social integration into the British way of life and their experiences. The impact that immigration rules have on minority ethnic groups varies according to the time of arrival, age and other varying circumstances. Thus, not all 'Black' people are affected by immigration reforms, although there are other issues affecting the Black African diasporic community that are also in need of favourable policy intervention. For instance, Black Britons might not be subject to immigration controls, but they are often acquainted with those who are, and the fact that you have a defined legal status in the UK is not sufficient to protect you from discrimination. It does not matter whether a person identifies as an African, Caribbean, or not; for a Black person, being 'British' is not always sufficient to protect one from the effects of racism and discrimination. Black Britons sometimes must contend with the limitations on fairness justice, diversity, inclusion and opportunities placed on them by society's stereotypes.

The limitations of this book should be explained from the onset. This is not a history book; the accounts of history are provided for illustrative purposes and as a form of addressing miseducation of today's black children. It also provides knowledge for anyone who is seeking to understand more about African history and their lived experience. This volume makes use of secondary literature when necessary, however, the vision for this work and much of the knowledge that is imparts is derived from the author's personal research and community engagement. This volume is thus a work in progress, and as such, none of the topics are exhaustive and conclusive. The author believes that the hostile environment created by new immigration policies indirectly impacts legal migrants and other ethnic minority communities within the diaspora by making their integration into the British community difficult. This book is self-funded by the author.

References

Alibhai-Brown, Y. (2015, 12 July). White people may deny it, but racism is back in Britain. *The Independent*. Retrieved from http://www.independent.co.uk/voices/comment/white-people-may-deny-it-but-racism-is-back-in-britain-10384129.html

Bulmer, M. (1996) The ethnic group question in the 1991 Census of Population, In Coleman, D & Salt, J. (Eds.). Ethnicity in the 1991 Census of Population, vol. 1 (pp. 33-62). London: HMSO.

Gardener, D., & Connolly, H. (2005). Who are the 'Other' ethnic groups? London: Office for National Statistics

Kaufmann, E. (2018). Why culture is more important than skills: Understanding British public opinion on immigration. LSE British Politics and Policy. London School of Economics and Political Science. Retrieved from http://blogs.lse.

ac.uk/politicsandpolicy/why-culture-is-more-important-than-skills-understanding-british-public-opinion-on-immigration/

Mazrui, A.A. (2009, 12 December). Africans of the blood and Africans of the soil. *The Daily Monitor*. Retrieved from http://www.monitor.co.ug/OpEd/Commentary/689364-823414-3jjhau/index.html

Slawson, N. (2017, 07 October). People from ethnic minorities still facing major jobs gap in UK. *The Guardian*. Retrieved from https://www.theguardian.com/world/2017/oct/07/ethnic-minorities-jobs-gap-bame-degrees

Woods, R. (2016, 01 June). England in 1966: Racism and ignorance in the Midlands. *BBC News: Birmingham & Black Country*. Retrieved from http://www.bbc.com/news/uk-england-birmingham-36388761

PART ONE

Purpose

This section of the volume 'Globalisation, human security and social inclusion' aims to counter misinformation about Africa by providing an overview of ancient African societies and the early African presence in Britain, as well as a discussion of Britain's interactions with Africa during the Trans-Atlantic Slave Trade and the period of African colonisation. The discussion includes reviews of African contributions to British development and military efforts.

Method/Approach

This study is informed by the use of primary and secondary historical sources, including such primary historical records as British church and government documents, compiled statistics, slave narratives and secondary reports and analyses by historians, archaeologists, sociologists, demographers, and other scholars who have examined pre-colonial and colonial African history and societies.

Findings

This study reveals the rich, underappreciated histories of ancient African societies, demonstrating that earlier interactions between Africans and Britain were complex and varied. It demonstrates that the racial and ethnic hierarchies that later came to divide British society were not instituted until the imposition of European dominance over Africa during the periods of enslavement and colonisation. Throughout these historical periods, Africans made enduring and lasting contributions to British social and economic development as well as the country's security. Moreover, the narratives of formerly enslaved Africans and the emergence of the Pan-African movement in the UK demonstrate that slavery and colonialism did not destroy Africans' capacity to achieve.

Originality/Value

African history remains under-explored, and the contributions of Africans to British wealth and social development remain underappreciated. These chapters provide a narrative that provides a detailed and intricate background of pre- and early modern African migrations to Britain and their roles in British society.

Chapter 1.

———~~~———

Black History or African History

One cannot talk about Black history without referencing Africa. Although Africa has played a role in human development from ancient times, its contribution has remained under-emphasised even today, over four decades after a month was dedicated to Black history in the UK. The precursors to Black History Month emerged from the work of historian Carter G. Woodson (1875-1950), who decried the political and economic oppression of Black Americans how it was reflected in the systematic exclusion of their achievements from the educational curriculum. Consequently, 'Negro History Week' was formulated in 1926 to celebrate African Americans achievements before, during, and after the institution of slavery and improve Black self-esteem, self- knowledge and contribute to meaningful education. Black History Month was declared an official annual celebration in the United States for the month of February by President Gerald Ford in 1976, and the celebration soon spread to Canada, the Netherlands and the United Kingdom.

Over 40 years have passed since Black History Month began to be celebrated in the United Kingdom. In the UK, the establishment of Black History Month was reportedly a response to the victimisation experienced by a Black student at school, who was unable to sleep one night and asked his mother, 'Mom, why can't I be white? '(Addai-Sebo, quoted in Vernon, 2017). Consequently, Akyaaba Addai-Sebo, then

3

the Special Projects Coordinator of the Ethnic Minorities Unit of the Greater London Council, initiated Black History Month (BHM) in the UK in 1977. The holiday provided an opportunity to educate communities about the history of Black people and their contributions to the U.K. and create an opportunity for communities to understand the diversity of cultures and thus foster community cohesion. It is now a common event that extends over the month of October and is commemorated with activities ranging from lectures, workshops, to celebrations of African cuisines, music, and other forms of entertainment.

It is a positive development that 'Black History Month' has been incorporated into the annual calendars of the public sector, many private organisations, local councils, and schools; however, more work remains to be done to ensure that the purpose for which Black History Month was initiated remains relevant to the needs it is meant to address. For example, as discussed further in chapter 5, the hostile environment introduced by then-Home Secretary Theresa May to address illegal immigration has also indirectly affected the ability of other non-White minorities to access services such as private renting or receive fair treatment in recruiting if their names sound 'foreign'.

This does not diminish the fact that there have been considerable improvements in the opportunities available to the Black, Asian and Minority Ethnics (BAME) groups in the UK. For example, there is a growing representation of BAME people within politics and also the public sector. However, these opportunities are not equal above all professions and this needs some improvement so that the diversity can be properly reflected. but there is evidence that The UK government audit released in October 2017 reported that ethnic minorities in Britain have fewer good outcomes than their white counterparts in the areas of criminal justice, health, education, employment, unemployment, and earnings (OurELBA, 2017).

Black History Month provides an opportunity to explore information about Black people and their contributions to the building of Britain. However, although this celebration of diversity has been incorporated into the annual calendar of most local councils and other public sectors within the UK, the contributions of people of African descent have largely remained minimised in British society. Stories of prominent Africans from 15th century Tudor England are rarely shared in the educational curriculum, nor are histories shared about the ancient kingdoms and civilisations in Africa that predated the slave trade and the European colonisation of that continent. However, it has been acknowledged that black soldiers fought on the side of Britain during its civil wars in the 19th century. For example, as recounted in greater detail in chapter 3, James Africanus Horton (1835-1883) was a surgeon, soldier, and political activist who originally came from Sierra Leone. Another African named James Durham was born in and served in the military services in the 18th century. Sergeant William Gordon was a Jamaican who also served in the army forces. There were also women such as the Jamaican Mary Seacole, who helped to look after wounded soldiers in the Crimean War.

Despite evidence that Black people fought on the side of Britain during its civil wars in the 19th century and had critical roles in the establishment of institutions such as the National Health Service (NHS), this recognition has not translated into equality in the everyday lives of average Black Britons in the UK. African immigrants have historically made contributions to the economic enrichment of Britain, which cut across various fields such as the sciences, academics, medicine, support services engineering, law, and politics. However, these achievements are rarely chronicled in major newspapers; though the media does not mind showcasing the African community in sports and entertainment, thus reinforcing the stereotyped impression that these are the only areas in which they excel.

Misinformation about Africa

Related to the dismissal of African contributions to British society is the wealth of misconceptions about the continent itself. Much misinformation about Africa has spread over the centuries of its interactions with Europe, which have extended into the present day. Africa is sometimes erroneously referred to as a country, rather than a continent made up of 55 countries, each with its own diverse experiences and political, economic and social constructions relevant to its people. Western media coverage about African countries is sometimes biased and does not always represent the daily realities of African communities. Interest in Africa is generally more focused on political crises, poverty and other negative developments that capture headlines. News of thousands of Africans fleeing to Europe have flooded the news media; however, these reports do not consider the areas of growth in many African states. Even some Africans still believe that Africa has always been impoverished and 'backward' and that the continent's relationship with Europe has always been based on asymmetrical dynamics of enslavement and colonisation. Many modern Africans did not know or understand the slave trade until the emergence of the 1970s epic emotive series *Roots*, which awakened them to the experiences of enslaved Africans.

However, the history of Africans is not solely a chronicle of enslavement and colonialism, although these were significant experiences that impacted the continent. A look at the historical past of Africans before colonialism shows the dynamism of their cultural- and socio-political systems, and a visit to some historical sites in Africa would reveal the wonders and beauty of places such as the pyramids of Giza and the ruins of Great Zimbabwe, the stunning scenery and rich wildlife of the Ngorongoro Crater, the majestic power of the Nile River, and a host of other natural and constructed wonders.

Africa is the second largest continent in the world after Asia and is covered with a richly varied topography ranging from tropics and dense rainforest to savannas and expansive deserts. Africans also has a great deal of mineral wealth, and its artisans traditionally smelted iron and other metals, created iron tools and weapons as well as glorious artworks and jewellery made of copper, brass and gold, and designed and built expansive cities, pyramids, and other monumental works. Africa is an ethnically diverse continent divided into four zones of North of Africa, East Africa, South Africa and West Africa, with varying political and social structures across and within the different countries. The continent is home to over a billion people and nearly 3,000 languages. Africans take pride in their dialectic languages, which often cut across national borders and are used as markers of regional and ethnic identity.

This chapter provides an overview of the group of people identified as Africans and their history with Britain. I examine the splendour of ancient African societies and demonstrate that Black people were a part of British history long before slavery. All through its history and into the present day, Black people have played a significant role in the development of Britain.

Ancient African States

Anthropologists have established that humanity originated in East Africa, as evidenced by skulls of modern Homo sapiens dating to over

195,000 years ago that have been found in Ethiopia. Historical and archaeological literature has proved that prehistoric African societies were as organised as any of the countries in the Old World. Though many have assumed that sub-Saharan African states did not emerge until at least the 2nd millennium AD, it is now acknowledged that the northeast kingdoms of Punt and Kush interacted closely with Ancient Egypt. The kingdom of Punt, also called Pwenet or Pwene, and known to the Greeks as known to the Greeks as Opone (Mark, 2011), is believed to have been in Eritrea and/or Somalia. Punt was documented as a trading partner and source of cultural and religious influence for Egypt in the 3rd and 2nd millennia BCE, when the kingdom exported gold, ivory, ebony wood, wild animals and aromatic resins to Egypt in exchange for jewellery, tools, and weapons (Mark, 2011; Watterson, 1997). The Nubian state of Kush, located at the confluences of the Nile Rivers and the River Atbara in what are now the countries of Sudan and South Sudan, became independent from Egypt in the 11th century BCE and invaded that state in the 8th Century BCE, ruling there as pharaohs of the 25th Dynasty. Kush's kingdom, centred first at Napata and later in Meroe, built monumental temples, developed an indigenous alphabet by the early 2nd century BCE and endured until the 4th century AD (Török, 1997). Later, the Ethiopian/Eritrean kingdom of Aksum conquered the declining Kush state and flourished from 100 AD – 940 AD as a major player in the politics and trade of the Arabian Peninsula and in the commercial routes extending between India and the Roman Empire. The Aksumites built monumental palaces and tombs and established their own alphabet and currency. In the 3rd century, the Persian religious leader Mani considered Aksum to be among the four great powers of his time, with Persia, China and Rome as its only peers (Munro-Hay, 1991).

In the west, the roots of the Soninke or Sarakulle state of Ghana or Wagadou, which is chronicled as the first empire of West Africa (McKissack & McKissack, 1993), extend to the 2nd millennium BC in the African Sahel (Holl, 1985). Ghana expanded between 700 AD and the 13th century in what is now south-eastern Mauritania, Western Mali, and Eastern Senegal, and was later succeeded by the Mali and Songhay states. The economies of these empires thrived off commerce in salt, kola nuts, and gold; their kings entertained numerous foreign dignitaries and merchants, among whom they were renowned for their enormous wealth (Loimeier, 2003; Davidson, 2015). In the 14th century, Mali was listed with China and Iran as one of the world's top three richest countries. Mansa Musa (c. 1280—c. 1337), an emperor of Mali who became well known worldwide after travelling through North Africa and parts of the Middle East during his pilgrimage to Mecca, was worth over USD $400 billion in today's currency (Davidson, 2015). Timbuktu, an important city of Mali located about 12 miles north of the Niger River, was known as the 'city of gold' and had a population of over 115,000 people, as well as being home to West Africa's first university and extensive libraries full of hundreds of thousands of books on such topics as maths, medicine, poetry, law, and astronomy (Jones, 2013).

In the south, the kingdom of Zimbabwe, centred at the city of Great Zimbabwe, was a testimony to the flourishing of the Shona civilisation between the 11th and 15th centuries AD. The stone city of Great Zimbabwe, which archaeological evidence indicates was a thriving commercial centre, extended over an area of 7.22 kilometres and at its peak is believed to have housed a population of over 18,000 people. Great Zimbabwe comprised three major areas, namely the Hill Complex, the Valley Complex, and the Great Enclosure, and its ruins contained numerous carved stone artefacts, Chinese pottery, ivory and bronze weapons, copper smelting materials, Arabian coins, and various pieces of gold jewellery and regalia. In the 19ᵗʰ and 20ᵗʰ centuries, the site suffered much damage from the crude diggings by British colonialists, as well as others who mined the ruins for gold (Kaarsholm, 1992). The city's indigenous African origins have only been officially acknowledged in recent decades, as the British colonial Rhodesian government censored archaeologists who disputed the official narrative that the site was built by non-Black people (Garlake, 2002).

Indigenous Education

Most African indigenous education was a lifelong process of learning, whereby a person progressed through defined stages of the life from infancy through adulthood to the grave (Cameron & Dodd, 1970). Youth learned vital skills and knowledge through instruction by the older and more experienced members of the society. This ancient form of education was premised on five categories, namely the extended family, parents, grandparents, elders and the peer/age group (Mosha, 2000). African education taught that the extended family unit was an agent of education, whereby the family was a child's gateway to the world. Thus, children were brought up to respect parents, uncles, grandparents, and elders, who included other family members and friends, and any adult had the authority to correct a child that deviated from expected behaviours. Africans still emphasise the importance of the family life through proverbs. For example, the Yoruba of Nigeria have a saying: 'a man's legs are his brother and sister. On what else can he rely?' and the Ashanti people of Ghana believe that 'the ruin of a nation begins in the homes of its people' (Smith, 1992).

Parents were vested with the responsibility of teaching and guiding their children. Mothers spent more time with young children, whereas fathers supported the family economically. Children were taught to respect their parents and abide by their words, and parents were meant to show guidance and discipline. Thus, the relationship between parents and children were one of learning and training. As a Senegalese proverb describes the bond, 'if your son laughs when you scold him, you ought to cry for you have lost him; if he cries you may laugh for you have a worthy heir'. Thus, African societies traditionally upheld education oriented toward character building and the formation of the individual (Diop, 1987). Schooling did not occur within the four walls of a building as in European societies; rather, African children were taught how to survive and progress through experiences and instructions recounted by elders and adapting those teachings to their lives and environment. Children were given a form of education designed to prepare them to become responsible and productive community members upon adulthood.

African indigenous education was often more practical than Western forms; however, more specialised forms of learning were also available. For example, young adults developed skills in masonry, pottery making, carving, house-building, sculpting, canoe making, cloth making, and other technical crafts. The training in the skills required for activities such as masonry, medicine and iron smelting and blacksmithing was intensive and highly specialised, and many young adults were also taught subjects such as maths, agriculture and animal husbandry, history, religion, and law. Young adults were also trained for leadership. Among the Bena society in south-central Tanzania, for example, young adults who had demonstrated the appropriate skills and character development were sent to learn and work with chiefs and community leaders (Mushi, 2009). In more complex societies, exceptionally intelligent youth could receive intensive training in the use of proverbs, which were utilised in law, or be educated in diplomacy or to work in other court offices, such as administrators of the treasury, which in the case of the Akan-speaking peoples required knowledge of the mathematics of weights and measures to supervise the storage and apportionment of gold dust.

Precolonial African Universities

It is often assumed that there was no higher education in Africa before colonialism, and when higher education was eventually introduced, it declined after independence, causing many to look for alternatives abroad. Although it is true that much of African indigenous education was considered less formal, as can be seen above, many societies indeed developed other, more specialised forms of education, and in a few cases, university systems even emerged.

History reports that three forms of traditional institutions were established in Africa, namely the early Christian monasteries, the Alexandria Museum and Library, and the Islamic mosque universities. The Alexandria Museum was a well-reputed citadel of learning in 3rd century Egypt, and its library boasted of major volumes of collections. The museum housed more than 200,000 volumes and supported up to 5,000 scholars and students. Many leading Egyptian, Roman, Greek, Jewish and other African scholars studied there, and some worked in the various libraries within the museum. By the 4th century, following the development of Christianity in Ethiopia, monastic education began to flourish in that country as well (Zeleza, 2006). The schools were organised in a hierarchy, with the Qine Bet (School of Hymns) at the bottom, followed by the Zema Bet (School of Poetry, and at the then the Metsahift Bet (School of the Holy Books;

Zeleza, 2006). However, education in Ethiopia was largely restricted to the clergy and nobility until after the 12th century. Later, the monastic educational structure formed the basis of the state educational system, and subjects such as religious studies, philosophy, history and the computation of time and calendar were among the various subjects taught.

The Islamic form of higher education has been described as the highest form of schooling in Africa. The Arabic institutions boasted of three main universities as early as 732, such as Ezzitouna Madrasa in Tunis, University of al-Qarawiyyin, which was founded in 859 as the first degree-awarding educational institution in the world and remains the oldest continually operating university ('Medina of Fez', 1992-2018). There was also Al-Alzhar University, which was established in Cairo in 969 and attracted some of the greatest intellectuals of the Muslim world, including Ibn Khaldun, who was also a lecturer in the institution. Later, the city of Timbuktu in the Mali Empire boasted three centres of learning at the mosques of Sankore, Djinguereber, and Sidi Yahya. Sankore Madrasa, founded in 989 AD, was especially respected throughout the Islamic world and housed up to 25,000 students (Hunwick & Boye, 2008). In addition to religious education, these institutions offered courses such as logic, astronomy, history, astrology, geography, linguistics, physics, chemistry and philosophy, among other subjects (Hunwick & Boye, 2008). Students at the university earned General Studies degrees, which were centred on the basic sciences, while more specialised scholars earned a Superior Degree or could aspire to the level of Judge or Professor. The university's golden age lasted from the 12th to 16th centuries, but the institution went into decline upon the invasion of the Songhay Empire in the late 17th century, when many of its scholars were arrested, killed or exiled for 'disloyalty' (Hunwick, 2003).

Other precolonial Islamic universities also emerged in East Africa as Arabic traders began trading and intermarrying with populations along the coast. A number of universities in both East and West Africa have survived into the present, though they have changed over the centuries to imbibe some western course forms, including more secular, technical and professional fields of study. Many of these universities also became privatised as the support they got from the state became reduced.

Africa and Britain's Historical Relationship

African societies had engaged in various commercial partnerships with Europe for centuries before the colonial period began. West African nations such as Asante, Fante, Benin, Dahomey, and Yoruba established diplomatic ties and traded with England in gold, salt and other commodities as well as slaves. In the east, the British traded with the Buganda kingdom and the Arab empire based in Zanzibar. In the south, they dealt with the precolonial polities of the Ndebele and the Shona, successors to the Ancient Zimbabwe state.

The Asante State

The Asante are one of many Akan, or Twi-speaking people dispersed through the forest and forest-savannah fringes of modern Ghana, Togo, and Ivory Coast. The archaeological record and ethno-historical shows the Akan-speakers to have emerged out of a mixture of migrants from the Western Sudan (exiles from the declining Ancient Ghana Empire, according to some accounts) and communities largely indigenous to the area, with connections to the Kintampo farming complex that emerged between 2500-1400 BCE, and to Ghana's Early Iron Age societies of the early centuries AD. The first Akan state was ruled by the Bono of the present-day Brong-Ahafo region of Ghana, whose capital emerged as a major player in the trans-Saharan trade in the 13th-14th centuries (Effah-Gyamfi, 1985). The roots of the Asante Kingdom extend to the 9th-10th centuries AD at forest town of Asantemanso in Ghana. Oral traditions state that the ancestress Aberewa Samanto of the Royal Aduana clan emerged there from a hole in the earth, accompanied by her brother, Kwasi Aduaku, and other relations, who became the founding clans of the Asante (Shinnie & Shinnie, 1995). Archaeological evidence indicates that for a short time, Asantemanso was a commercial centre that prospered from its pottery and iron working industries; however, by around the 15th century, the town's fortunes had declined, and the Asante dispersed to various areas north, yet remained in the forest zones.

The Asante Empire was founded in 1670 by the legendary priest Okomfo Anokye, who created the Golden Stool that is said to hold the spirit of the Asante people, and the king Osei Tutu. The capital was established at Kumase ten years later, and its strategic location on a crossroads of the trans-Saharan trade routes ensured its prosperity. Over the next few decades, the Asante subdued the neighbouring Akan states, defeating their overlords the Denkyira in 1701 and expanding outward from Kumase to encompass the Brong-Ahafo areas on the fringes of the savannah to the north, into what are now Togo and Ivory Coast to the east and west, respectively, and south to the coast, where they often superseded local groups such as the Ewe, Ga or Fante-Akans and traded with the Dutch and other European powers (McCaskie, 1995). Ashanti's Foreign Office ministry was divided into several departments, each of which functioned separately to handle relations between the Empire and diplomats representing the British, French, Dutch, and various Arab and other Muslim nations, respectively (McCaskie, 1995). The British had arrived at the coastal areas of Ghana in the 16th century, establishing close relations with the Fante-Akan and bringing home its first shipment of gold in 1553. In 1651, Britain built a coastal fort at Kormantine, and another at Cape Coast ten years later. Whereas the British and other European nations largely dominated affairs among coastal groups, they were forced to deal with the Asante more or less as equals, establishing diplomats and only passing along the Asante's well-maintained road system with the permission of the forest kingdom.

By the early 19th century, having all but taken over the coastal lands of the Fante, the Ga and the Ewe, the British had begun to penetrate the forests, but their forces were fiercely resisted by the Asante, who were themselves expanding south to the coastal areas and generally prevailed over their early disputes. In all, a series of five Anglo-Asante Wars were fought between 1823 and 1901. Though the Asante were able to stop earlier British attempts to move north into its territory, a shift began from 1867, when the British Gold Coast was formally established, and the third Anglo-Asante War ended with a decided Asante defeat, and the kingdom was forced to settle hostilities by paying 50,000 ounces of gold, allowing the British to trade freely on the coast, and keeping a major road to Kumase open to the British at all times (Edgerton, 1995). The fourth war with Asante ended with the kingdom being named a British Protectorate in 1897. After a final uprising in 1902, which was precipitated by the demand of the British representative for the Golden Stool to sit on and led by Yaa Asantewaa, the *Asantehemma* (Queen-Mother) of Ejisu, many members of the royal family were exiled to the Seychelles as the kingdom was fully incorporated into the British Colony of the Gold Coast.

The Yoruba States

The lands of the Yoruba-speaking peoples, who are currently numbered at around 30 million, span the southern areas of modern Togo, Benin and Nigeria. Their historical roots extend to settlements associated with early Yoruba speakers dating to the 4th century BC at their ancestral centre of Ile-Ife in southwestern Nigeria and other nearby sites. Historical evidence indicates that the town was first established by the *Oba* (divine king) Oduduwa, whose armies drove out the earlier Igbo settlements in the area to establish the first Yoruba kingdom and begin spreading north, west and east throughout the wider Niger River area. Between 700 and 900 AD, the city began to develop as an artistic hub, and by the 12th century, Ife had developed into an urban centre of substantial size, the inhabitants of which resided in houses fronted by potsherd pavements and were engaged in a thriving and refined sculptural tradition based on naturalistic works produced from terracotta, stone, and copper alloys. By the 15th century, however, Ife's pre-eminence had begun to decline as it was eclipsed by centres such as Benin (see below) and Oyo.

Oyo Ile, which emerged as an urban centre around the 12th century AD, had established itself as a formidable power by the 15th century, and after recovering from a military defeat by the nearby Nupe polity in the mid-16th century (Stride & Ifeka, 1971), Oyo grew to become the dominant political and military power of Yorubaland by the end of the 17th century, establishing and controlling a vast empire of over 150,000 square kilometres, an area that encompassed a number of subordinate city-states between the savannah plains of present-day Northcentral Nigeria and the forests of Southwest Nigeria and the Niger River (Thornton, 1998). Oyo's only serious opposition in the region was from the Dahomey and Benin kingdoms; whereas the latter was never conquered and remained separated from Oyo by a buffer area settled by non-Yoruba speakers to the southeast, Oyo finally succeeded in forcing Dahomey to pay it tribute in 1748 (Stride & Ifeka, 1971).

A major source of wealth for Oyo came from its slave dealings with British and other European traders. Though previous kings had preferred to focus on gaining wealth through military expansion, their dealings in the slave trade expanded dramatically when the trader Abiodun became *alafin* (king) in 1770, and within two years the Oyo-controlled Porto Novo had become the leading port for the slave trade (Lovejoy, 2012). During the latter half of the 18th century, Oyo began to lose influence as city-states such as Ilorin began to secede, emboldened by the infighting that had begun among the weakening rulership. Its collapse grew more imminent after the British, who by then had become their main trading partners, outlawed the slave trade in 1807, unsettling Oyo's economy significantly (Metz, 1991). In 1823, Dahomey defied Oyo by raiding villages for slaves to trade with Europeans, and decisively resisted Oyo's attempts at chastisement. The empire finally collapsed after the invasion and sacking of Oyo Ile by the Islamic Fulani Empire in 1823, and though the capital was moved, Oyo's days as a regional power had effectively ended, and it was forced to compete with other powerful Yoruba states such as Ibadan, Ijaye and Ilorin. British dealings with the kingdom intensified as its hegemony weakened. In the 1830s, the first Christian missionaries arrived in the area, spearheaded by ex-slaves from the region who had been converted to the religion, such as Samuel Ajayi Crowther, a Yoruba born in the Egba (Igbo) settlement of Osogun who had been captured along with his entire village at the age of 12 by Oyo and Fulani raiders and sold to Portuguese traders before his slave ship was boarded by a British Royal Ship and he was released and resettled in Sierra Leone (Walls, 1998). Crowther later led a British Christian mission to the Niger in 1841 to spread commerce and Christianity, teach agricultural techniques, and help end the slave trade. After the slave trade began to decline, much of the commerce by Oyo, Ibadan and other Yoruba kingdoms focused on the purchase of British firearms, which they used to war against each other, thus further weakening their ability to resist British incursions (Beck, 2010). The British actively encouraged such competition, smuggling arms to some groups and blockading others. By the 1850s, the British had begun to destroy Yoruba towns and annex others as part of its colony, and by the time of the Berlin Conference of 1885, they effectively controlled the entire southern Niger region (Beck, 2010).

The Benin Kingdom

The Benin kingdom emerged during the 13th century in what is now the Edo state in southwest Nigeria. Oral traditions report that the Binis had migrated from Egypt after short sojourns in Sudan and Ile-Ife in search of new lands in which to settle (Egharevba, 1960). Benin was renowned for its antiquity and civilisation on the banks of the Niger and was reportedly once the most powerful state in West Africa (Egharevba, 1960). The empire included numerous towns and villages with hereditary chiefs, and its artisans were famed for their technical mastery, particularly in the casting of bronze sculptures. Oral tradia tions identify its first rulers as Edo people from the Ogiso (Kings of the Sky) dynasty founded in 900AD, who called their kingdom Igodomigodo (Egharevba, 1960). In the 12th century, however, that dynasty ended after a power struggle, and the rulers went into exile at the Yoruba kingdom at Ile Ife. After that, the Edo people appear to have come under the influence of Ife, as oral traditions state that they allowed Prince Oranmiyan, son of the exiled Ogiso, to rule them. Facing local resistance, Oranmiyan eventually resigned his office and returned to Ile Ife, and his son Eweka, whose mother was from Edo, became the first King, or *Oba*, of Benin (Egharevba, 1960). Though Benin became an independent kingdom, its rulers retained the Yoruba title of *Oba*, and though those links are currently disputed on both sides, *Oba*s of Benin have maintained ritual ties to Ile Ife to this day.

By the mid-15th century, Benin had completely broken away from Ife's hegemony and expanded its rule to take on imperial status. Its capital, Benin City, was centred by a monumental palace with a collection of buildings that were well built and close to each other (Egharevba, 1960). In the words of the Dutch physician and explorer Olfert Dapper (1668), 'these people are in no way inferior to the Dutch as regards cleanliness; they wash and scrub their houses so well that they are polished and shining like a looking glass'. Ethno-mathematician Ron Eglash (1999) noted that Benin City and its surrounding villages and towns were in fact laid out to form perfect fractals, with each of the capital's 11 divisions duplicating the design of the king's court. In the houses, similar shapes were repeated in the rooms, and the houses and clusters of houses in the settlements were arranged in mathematically predictable patterns.

Benin's interactions with Europeans began in 1480 with the arrival of the Portuguese to their lands, and over the next two centuries, the kingdom also engaged in commerce with merchants from France, Spain, Germany and England. In the 17th-18th centuries, Benin controlled most of the trade in slaves along the entire coastline from the Western Niger Delta to the Akan areas of modern-day Ghana, conquering the Lagos lagoon in Nigeria, which they called Eko, and establishing a major trading post there in the 16th century. Lagos served as a major centre for the slave trade. There was ongoing trade between the Benin Kingdom and the British, who gradually displaced the other European powers in the area; however, Benin's control of these markets began to decline as the kingdom became embroiled in civil wars during the mid-18th century. In 1841, Oba Akitoye was dethroned by local merchants and exiled after attempting to ban the slave trade, and only succeeded in regaining his position with the assistance of British authorities, thus enhancing their influence in the kingdom. The British annexed Lagos as its colony in 1861 and took control of other parts of modern-day Nigeria in 1887, though the kingdom managed to retain independence and exercise a monopoly over trade. However, in the late 19th century, *Oba* Ovonramwen Nogbaisi imposed customs duties on goods leaving the territory. Taking umbrage at this restriction, the British sent a troop of about 1,200 soldiers to destroy the kingdom (Egharevba, 1960), taking over the city of Benin in February 1897, raiding houses and burning the palace and city to the ground. During the raid, the British troops sacked a large collection of the famed Benin bronze artefacts from the King's palaces, and they were placed in the British Museum in London.

The Buganda Kingdom

The name 'Uganda' was used by Arab and Swahili traders from the East African coast to refer to the kingdom of Buganda, which they encountered in the interior in the mid-nineteenth century. Buganda's ruling dynasty extends to the 14th century, when founding *Kabaka* (king) Kato Kintu, said to have been an exiled prince, invaded the area with a large force and established hegemony over the loosely united clans after defeating their leader, Bemba. Local clan leaders allied themselves with the new king, and together they established the system of laws, hierarchies and clan relationships now known as the Buganda Constitution. Kato Kintu established his palace along the shore of Lake Victoria (which the Ganda called Nnalubale) at Nnono. Beginning in the 16th century, the Buganda expanded their kingdom from three to twelve provinces with the aid of their mastery of black-smithing techniques, shifting their capital to Lubaga and conquering the surrounding kingdoms to establish a territory encompassing all of what is now central Uganda. By the 18th century, Buganda had eclipsed the formerly dominant Bunyoro kingdom, and by the time of the arrival of Arab and Swahili traders seeking ivory and slaves in the 1840s, it was among the most powerful states in East Africa.

The British first arrived to the area in the 1860s. In 1875, the British journalist Henry Morton Stanley marvelled at the size of the Buganda army, which he numbered at about 125,000 forces and was support-ed by a royal navy of outrigger canoes commanded by an admiral, as well as the capital, a well-ordered town of about 40,000 people centred at the king's palace, which was situated atop a commanding hill and surrounded by a wall of more than four kilometres in circum-ference. With the arrival of French and British Christian missionaries in the 1880s, Buganda developed a thriving textile industry based on the addition to cotton to its other crops, such as maize and bananas. However, after the untimely death of the strong and powerful King Mutesa I in 1884 just a few years after the arrival of the missionaries, he was succeeded by the much weaker king Mwanga II, who aroused the anger of the Europeans and undermined local support by having a number of the missionaries and their Bagandan converts arrested and executed. By 1888, the British had firmly set their sights on Buganda as part of its expanding sphere of interest in the area and set up the Imperial British East Africa Company to administer the territory. Caught between the French, British and Germans, the Buganda, under the rule of their new and weaker leader, soon succumbed to European rule, first agreeing to become a German Protectorate in 1890 before becoming a British Protectorate in 1894. Unlike they did with the Asante and Benin kingdoms in the West, the British, appeased by the ceding of power by the kingdom's ruler, recognised the status of the *Kabaka* and his ruling chiefs, permitting them to retain control of their territories and essentially using them to administer the area and supervise the growing of cotton by the local peasant farmers.

Overview of Early African Migrations to Britain

The displacement of peoples and individuals is an experience common to all nations, and Africa is not an exception. Of course, Africans were the world's first migrants, as the first modern humans moved out of that continent into Asia and Europe tens of thousands of years in the past. Later historical African migrations were also different from contemporary migrations in the sense that traditionally, migrations involved discovering new places of settlement, where Africans would establish villages and societies with organised structures (Baker & Aida, 1995). Based on the nomadic and semi-nomadic lifestyles of some early African societies, it was relatively easy for them to travel in small groups and form communities. Before European colonisation, Africa was marked by many great movements of peoples; however, it was only in contemporary times that the trend of African migration shifted to become movements of labour. People now move from rural to urban zones in search of sustainable employment, from towns to cities, and from country to country, and in the last decades, movements of people have again included international migration.

Black people were a part of British history long before slavery. A recent DNA analysis of ancient remains has revealed the presence of dark-skinned peoples who most certainly would be called 'Black' today among Britain's earliest inhabitants. A forensic analysis of the famous 'Cheddar Man' fossil, which dates to about 10,000 years ago, indicated that along with blue eyes, he had 'dark to black' skin and dark, curly hair (Devlin, 2018). The Cheddar man fossil shares many genetic traits with 'other dark-skinned individuals from the Mesolithic era found in Spain, Hungary, and Luxemborg' (Gibbens, 2018). Mid-20th century osteo-archaeological excavations have revealed a definite Black African presence in Britain in approximately 245 AD, as evidenced by the remains of a Black woman Briton of sub-Saharan African descent named the 'Beachy Head Lady' after the East Sussex beauty spot where she was discovered, who is believed to have held a prominent position in the Roman-British society of the period (Zolfagharifard, 2014). In 2010, isotopic and skull morphology analyses identified another woman of sub-Saharan African descent, now called 'the ivory bangle lady', as having been among the wealthiest residents of York in the 4th century AD; she was interred in a stone sarcophagus along with a number of luxury items, including bracelets of African ivory and Yorkshire jet, a mirror, and a glass perfume jar (Kennedy, 2010). Other evidence indicates the presence of African men in Roman Britain, some of whom were likely enslaved, although archaeological inscriptions have revealed that more than one unit of North African soldiers, some of whom were high-ranking, to have been stationed at forts on Hadrian's Wall (Benjamin & Greaves, 2001). Another prominent African Briton, Hadrian, who was a 7th century abbot of St Peter's and St Paul's at Canterbury, was described as 'vir natione Afir' (a man of the African race), and notes on his teachings include vocabulary and references that have led many historians to believe that he was of Libyan descent (Hudson, 2016). Having rejected the role of Archbishop for himself, Hadrian was sent to England by Pope Vitalian as an assistant to the newly appointed Archbishop of Canterbury, where he is said to have played a critical role in the development of religious structures in England and may have also influenced Anglo-Saxon literature (Hudson, 2016).

Not all Africans in earlier British history were of higher social status. In 862 AD, the Annals of Ireland recorded that enslaved Africans (called 'blue men' in the Irish and Norse languages) were brought to their shores by Vikings returning from raids on Spain and North Africa, and the skeletal remains of one bonded or enslaved Black girl were identified in a 10th century Anglo-Saxon burial at North Elmham in Norfolk (Edwards 1981). The skeletal remains of another possibly enslaved young African woman who lived during the same time period were found in Gloucestershire River in Fairford; based on the nearly intact condition of the bones, it is believed that she might have been buried nearby and came to be exposed through erosion (Archer, 2013). Later, an entry for Derbyshire dating to c. 1241 in The Domesday Abbrevia, a survey of English landholders and boroughs originally ordered by William the Conqueror, is illustrated with a capital letter 'I' that is held by a Black man whose attire has been associated with peasant or labourer status (The National Archives, n.d.). On the other hand, forensic analysis of a skeleton buried at the Greyfriars monastery identified the 'Ipswitch Man' as a North African buried there in the latter half of the 13th century. He appears to have suffered from a spinal abscess, and his burial in a single grave, rather than a common plot, as well as historical records documenting the use of the monasteries as paid hospices by many during that time, has been interpreted as a strong suggestion that he was neither poor nor enslaved (Black, 2010).

Contrary to sources identifying Africans in Tudor England mostly as servants and slaves, more recent scholarship has argued that these Africans brought valuable skills with them, and some of were also visiting dignitaries (Nubia, 2012). Many of these Africans were from the Northern part of Africa in Morocco, whereas others hailed from post-Moorish Spain or West Africa (Kaufmann, 2017). The status of some of the North Africans who visited and were in Tudor England is explained in the following statement:

Some North Africans certainly visited England. The King of Morocco's ambassador, who arrived with a retinue of fifteen 'Moors', was given a warm reception by Elizabeth in 1600. Nevertheless, they had trouble obtaining housing. When they did find accommodation, they lived alone and were 'strangely attired and behaviours', and reputedly slaughtered their animals [presumably to fulfil religions requirements] (Sherwood, 2003).

Historical records document a number of Africans present in Tudor England in the 15th and 16th centuries, who lived in the cities of London, Plymouth and Bristol, as well as such towns and villages as Blean in Kent, Hatherleigh in Devon, Holt in Worcestershire and Salisbury in Wiltshire (Kaufmann, 2017). A few of these people were part of the entourage of Catherine of Aragon in 1507, such as Iberian Moor Catalina de Cardones, who arrived in England in 1501 and served as Catherine's lady of the bedchamber (Nubia, 2012). John Blanke, a Black trumpeter, was employed by Henry VII and Henry VIII from 1506–12 and lived in London in 1507 (Nubia, 2012). Though Queen Elizabeth I signed two letters in 1596 written by merchants deploring the excessive numbers of Black people in England, she is also documented as having had at least one African in her personal entourage – 'a Blackamoore boy', who is mentioned in a warrant ordering him an outfit of fine clothing dated 14 April 1574 (Kaufmann, 2017). Less prominent Black Africans present in England during the Elizabethan period and located through Baptismal records include Mary Fillis, a Moroccan who came to England with her father from Andalusia, worked as a seamstress and was baptised at St. Botoph's, Aldgate in London in 1597 (Wood, 2012). Burial records at St. Botolphs, Aldn gate also include Christopher Cappervert, a 'Blackemoore' from Cape Verde (1586), Symon Valencia (1593) and Cassangoe (1593) ('Black and Asian people discovered in records held by the Manuscripts Section', 2009). David Olusoga has argued that Black history did not only involve Black people, but also included encounters between Blacks and Whites, including intermarriage or other mixed relationships (Olusoga, 2016; Wood, 2012). It was common during the Elizabethan period for Black people to marry whites, such as the case of 'Reasonable Blackman', a silk weaver living in Southwark near London Bridge from 1579-1592, who married an English wife around 1587 (Wood, 2012).

Outside of London, records document the names of about ten Africans living in Southampton, one of whom was called Jacques Francis, a notable diver who assisted in the search for the wreck of the Mary Rose, Henry VIII's great warship, which sunk in 1545, and who later became the first known African to give evidence in an English court of law (Kaufmann, 2017). Some Black servants are even known to have delivered physical discipline against Britons. In 1596 in rural Gloucestershire, a man of African descent named Edward Swarthye, who was educated in Latin, Greek and French and served as porter to Sir Edward Wynter, was recorded as having publicly whipped another high-ranking servant on his lord's behalf (Kaufmann, 2017). That chastised servant was John Guye, who then ran Wynter's ironworks, but was later to become the first English governor of Newfoundland. Another Black person living in rural Gloucestershire was a woman named Cattalena, who lived independently in Almondsbury, profiting off of milk and butter sales to her neighbours until her death in 1625. Many Africans working in England were sailors and Kaufmann (2017) has pointed out that of the 100 sailors on Blackbeard's flagship in the early 18th century, nearly two-thirds were Black.

One cannot deny that a larger influx of Black Africans arrived in Britain as captives. As far back as 1554, a group of five Africans were 'seized' from the Gold Coast (now Ghana) to learn English so they could act as interpreters in their homeland as part of the British effort to consolidate their interests in West Africa and break the Portuguese monopoly over the slave trade (Dakubu, 1997). However, members of their local communities kept track of their progress, and few years later, they returned home to be employed as free men. In a similar case, a Khoikhoi man named Coree was seized from near the Cape of Good Hope by the East India Company in 1613 and brought to London to be lodged with a merchant from that company and provide information to aid them with their commercial ventures (Fryer, 1984). Coree assisted the company with their trading ventures, and was bribed liberally to -accept his condition, and when he was finally returned home to appease the protests of his country folk, he continued to work for the English as a middleman between them and his people (Fryer, 1984). On one occasion, Coree reported that the Europeans were offering trading stock that they little valued, recommending that the Africans raise their prices so as to better profit from their dealings with them (Kaufmann, 2017).

Others, however, were not forcibly taken by the English, but were rather sent to England by African rulers who sought similar advantages. Dederi Jaquoah, the son of Cadidi-biah, ruler of a territory located between present-day Sierra Leone and Liberia that traded in ivory and meleguetta pepper, was sent to London by his father in 1610 to learn about the English in anticipation of developing a trading partnership. Dederi converted to Christianity in 1611, and remained in London for two years, living with a merchant, observing local ways and working as a translator before returning home to manage his father's trading interests (Kaufmann, 2017).

Conclusion

This chapter has attempted to address negative stereotypes about Africa, its history, and its people by examining the splendour of pre-colonial African states, the history of African interactions with Britain, and markers of the early African presence in this country. It has demonstrated that while slavery and colonialism are inextricably woven into Africa's later history, the foundations of African cultural, economic and political development extend much further back in time, and the first encounters between African migrants and Britain were grounded in significantly more balanced and equitable relations than is acknowledged today. Nations such as Morocco, Asante, Benin and Buganda did not approach Britain as supplicants; rather, they were themselves approached by Britain, which sought alliances in their struggles against other European nations as well as to profit from the expansive wealth of African societies.

Accounts of African history have tended to be accompanied by a great deal of misinformation and prejudiced ideas due to the continent's involvement in the Atlantic slave trade and colonisation (Smythe, 2015). Africa was once dubbed the 'Benighted continent', the 'Benighted land' or the 'Dark Continent', and has been regarded as impenetrable, mysterious, underdeveloped, inadequately explored, remote from the rest of the world, bountiful in vegetation and wild animals and sparsely inhabited (Musere, 2016). As people, Africans have been labelled as poorly enlightened and un-progressive: perceptions both form the way Africans are seen by foreigners and influence the way Africans see themselves.

It was long assumed that Africa had never evolved worthwhile histories or civilisations of their own, but rather lived in a state of chaos and social and technological stagnation until the coming of Europeans (Davidson, 1959). As Mawuena Kossi Logan lamented (1999, p. 22), 'it is a paradox that in the fifteenth century, when Europe was about to embark on its sea voyages of explorations and conquest, Africans, who were far from being backwards, would be chained and shipped to the New World as slaves'. Yet, as Roland Oliver and J.D. Fage argued (1962, p. 14), '[i]n pre-historic times-at least through all the long millennia of the Paleolithic or 'Old Stone Age'—Africa was not even relatively backward: it was in the lead'. The story of Africa has been embedded with various theories from past to present; however, one cannot deny that the African continent has helped shape the world as it is today, including present global economic and industrial systems.

The facts of African history need to be reinstated. In many African primary and secondary schools, children have been taught about the voyages of Christopher Columbus (1451-1506) and Mungo Park (1771-1806), while learning very little about the Egyptian pyramids and the expansive civilisations that predated colonial rule. In the same vein, many children know the stories of Tarzan and Jack and the Beanstalk but know nothing about African folklores and African folktales. A major aim of Black history studies in the United States has been to ensure the proper inclusion of Black history into general American history and spread knowledge about Blacks and their accomplishments and potential to benefit all of American society (Horne, 2015). Similarly, this recounting of African history and some early contributions of Black Africans to the UK is aimed at helping Black Britons understand the integral roles of their forebears in shaping, enriching, and protecting the political, economic, and social development of British society.

The next two chapters will continue this work by delving deeply into the history of Britain's role in the Transatlantic Slave Trade and in the Colonisation of Africa.

References

'Ancient Egyptian Calendar' (2017). Retrieved from http://www.historyembalmed. org/ancient-egyptians/ancient-egyptian-calendar.htm

Archer, M. (2013, 28 September). Historians give theories on how a 1,000-year-old African skeleton appeared in the River Coln, Fairford. *Wilts & Gloucestershire Standard*. Retrieved from http://www.wiltsglosstandard.co.uk/ news/10703029.Historians_give_theories_on_African_skeleton_mystery/

Beck, S. (2010). *Mideast and Africa 1700-1950*. Ethics of Civilization, Vol. 16. Santa Barbara, CA World Peace Communications.

Benjamin, R.P., & Greaves, A.M. (2001). The archaeology of Black Britain: approaches, methods and possible solutions. Case study: North African soldiers at Aballava (Burgh-by-Sands). Retrieved from https://blackpresence.co.uk/black-romans/

Black and Asian people discovered in records held by the Manuscripts Section (2009). Guildhall Library Manuscripts Section. Retrieved fromhttp://www.history.ac.uk/gh/baentries.htm

Black, S. (2010, 08 May). He was an African who had a strong jaw and a bad back... So what was he doing in Ipswich in the year 1190? *The Daily Mail*. Retrieved from http://www.dailymail.co.uk/sciencetech/article-1275339/He-African-strong-jaw-bad--So-doing-Ipswich-year-1190.html

Cameron, J., & Dodd, W.A. (1970). *Society, schools and progress in Tanzania*. Oxford, UK: Pergamon Press.

Dakubu, M.E.K. (1997). *Korle meets the sea: a sociolinguistic history of Accra*. Oxford, UK: Oxford University Press.

Davidson, B. (1959). *The lost cities of Africa*. Boston, MA: Little, Brown.

Davidson, J. (2015, July 30). The 10 richest people of all time. *Time Money*. Retrieved from http://time.com/money/3977798/the-10-richest-people-of-all-time/

Department of the Arts of Africa, Oceania, and the Americas. (2000). The Trans-Saharan gold trade (7th–14th century). In *Heilbrunn timeline of art history*. New York: The Metropolitan Museum of Art, 2000–. http://www.metmuseum.org/ toah/hd/gold/hd_gold.htm

Devlin, H. (2018, 07 February). First modern Britons had 'dark to black' skin, Cheddar Man DNA analysis reveals. *The Guardian*. Retrieved from https://www.

theguardian.com/science/2018/feb/07/first-modern-britons-dark-black-skin-cheddar-man-dna-analysis-reveals

Diop, C.A. (1987). *Precolonial Black Africa: a comparative study of the political and social systems of Europe and Black Africa, from Antiquity to the formation of modern states*. Westport, CT: Lawrence Hill & Co.

Effah-Gyamfi, K. (1985). *Bono Manso: an archaeological investigation into early Akan urbanism*. Calgary: Department of Archaeology, University of Calgary.

Egharevba, J. (1960). *A short history of Benin* (3rd ed.). Ibadan, NG: Ibadan University Press.

Eglash, R. (1999). *African fractals: modern computing and indigenous design*. New Brunswick, NJ: Rutgers University Press.

Fryer, P. (1984). *Staying power: the history of black people in Britain*. Edmonton: University of Alberta Press.

Garlake, P. (2002). *Early art and architecture of Africa*. Oxford, UK: Oxford University Press.

Gibbens, S. (2018, 07 February). Britain's dark-skinned, blue-eyed ancestor explained. *National Geographic*. Retrieved from https://news.nationalgeographic.com/2018/02/ancient-face-cheddar-man-reconstructed-dna-spd/

Hays, J. (2008). Ancient Egyptian architecture. Retrieved from http://factsanddetails.com/world/cat56/sub365/item1934.html

Holl, A. (1985). Background to the Ghana Empire: Archaeological investigation on the transition to statehood in the Dar Tichitt Region (Mauritania). *Journal of Anthropological Archaeology*, 4(2), 73-115.

Horne, D. (2015, 26 February). The effects of Black History Month. *Our Weekly*. Retrieved from http://ourweekly.com/news/2015/feb/26/effects-black-history-month/?page=2

Hudson, A. (2016, 27 October). An African Abbot in Anglo-Saxon England. Retrieved from http://blogs.bl.uk/digitisedmanuscripts/2016/10/an-african-abbot-in-anglo-saxon-england.html

Hunwick, J.O. (2003). *Timbuktu and the Songhay Empire: Al-Sadi's Tarikh al-Sudan down to 1613 and other contemporary documents*. Leiden, UK: Brill

Hunwick, J.O. & Boye, A.J. (2008). *The hidden treasures of Timbuktu: rediscovering Africa's literary culture*. New York, NY: Thames & Hudson

Jones, J. (2013, 28 January). Destruction of Timbuktu manuscripts is an offence against the whole of Africa. *The Guardian*. Retrieved from https://www.theguardian.com/world/2013/jan/28/destruction-timbuktu-manuscripts-offence-africa

Kaarsholm, P. (1992). The past as battlefield in Rhodesia and Zimbabwe. Collected Seminar Papers. Institute of Commonwealth Studies. 42, 156-170. Retrieved from http://sas-space.sas.ac.uk/4213/1/Preben_Kaarsholm_-_The_past_as_battlefield_in_Rhodesia_and_Zimbabwe.pdf

Kaufmann, M. (2017). *Black Tudors: the untold story*. London, UK: Oneworld Publications

Kennedy, M. (2010, 26 February). African origin of Roman York's rich lady with the ivory bangle. *The Guardian*. Retrieved from https://www.theguardian.com/science/2010/feb/26/roman-york-skeleton

Logan, M.K. (1999). *Narrating Africa: George Henty and the fiction of empire*. New York, NY: Garland.

Loimeier, R. (2003). *Muslim societies in Africa: a historical anthropology*. Bloomington, IN: Indiana University Press.

Lovejoy, P.E. (2012). *Transformations of Slavery: A History of Slavery in Africa*. London: Cambridge University Press.

Loyn, H.R. (1991). *Anglo-Saxon England and the Norman Conquest* (2nd ed.). London, UK: Longman.

Mark, J.J. (2011, 01 August). Punt. *The ancient history encyclopedia*. Retrieved from https://www.ancient.eu/punt/

Medina of Fez. (1992-2018). *UNESCO World Heritage Centre*. UNESCO. Retrieved from http://whc.unesco.org/en/list/170

McCaskie, T. (1995). *State and society in pre-colonial Asante*. Cambridge, UK: Cambridge University Press.

McKissack, P., & McKissack, F. (1993). *The royal kingdoms of Ghana, Mali, and Songhay*. New York, NY: Henry Holt & Company

Mosha, R.S. (2000). *The Heartbeat of Indigenous Africa: A Study of the Chagga Educational System*. New York: Garland Publishing, Inc.

Munro-Hay, S. (1991). *Aksum: An African civilisation of late antiquity*. Edinburgh: Edinburgh University Press.

Musere, J. (2016). *Africa the dark continent according to foreigners*. Los Angeles, CA: Ariko Publications.

Mushi P.A. K. (2009) *History of Education in Tanzania*. Dar-es-Salaam: Dar-es-Salaam University Press.

National Archives, The (n.d.). Domesday legacy. Retrieved from http://www.nationalarchives.gov.uk/domesday/discover-domesday/domesday-legacy.htm

Nubia, O. (2012, 27 July). The Missing Tudors: Black people in 16th-century England. *BBC History Magazine*. Retrieved fromhttp://www.historyextra.com/period/tudor/the-missing-tudors-black-people-in-16th-century-england/

Oliver, R., & Fage, J.D. (1962). *A short history of Africa*. Harmondsworth, UK: Penguin.

Olusoga, D. (2016). *Black and British: a forgotten history*. London, UK: Pan Macmillan.

OurELBA. (2017, 10 October). Government report shows major disadvantages facing ethnic minorities – what ELBA is doing about it. Retrieved from https://elba-1.org.uk/blog/government-report-shows-major-disadvantages-facing-ethnic-minorities-what-elba-is-doing-about-it/

Pelteret, D. A. E. (1995). *Slavery in early Mediaeval England: from the reign of Alfred until the twelfth century*. Studies in Anglo-Saxon history. Woodbridge, UK: Boydell Press.

Sherwood, M. (2003, 10 October). Black people in Tudor England. *History Today*, 53(10).

Shinnie, P. & Shinnie, A. (1995). *Early Asante*. Calgary: Department of Archaeology, University of Calgary.

Smith, W.S. (1958). *The art and architecture of Ancient Egypt*. Harmondsworth, UK: Penguin

Smythe, K. (2015). *Africa's past, our future*. Bloomington, IN: Indiana University Press.

Stride, G.T. & Ifeka, C. (1971). *Peoples and empires of West Africa: West Africa in history 1000-1800*. Edinburgh: Nelson

Thornton, J. (1998). *Africa and Africans in the making of the Atlantic world, 1400-1800* (2nd ed.). Cambridge: Cambridge University Press.

Török, L. (1997). *The Kingdom of Kush: handbook of the Napatan-Meriotic civilization*. New York, NY: Brill.

Vernon, P. (2017, 03 October). Akyaaba Addai-Sebo. Retrieved fromhttps://www.blackhistorymonth.org.uk/article/section/interviews/akyaaba-addai-sebo/

Walls, A.F. (1998) Crowther, Samuel Adjai (or Ajayi), in G.H. Anderson (Ed.), *Biographical Dictionary of Christian Missions* (pp. 160-161). New York: Macmillan Reference USA.

Watterson, B. (1997). *The Egyptians*. Hoboken, NJ: Wiley-Blackwell.

Wood, M. (2012, 20 July). Britain's first black community in Elizabethan London. *BBC News Magazine*. Retrieved from http://www.bbc.com/news/magazine-18903391

Zeleza, P.T. (2006, 30 August). Beyond Afropessimism: historical accounting of African Universities. *Pambazuka News*. Retrieved from https://www.pambazuka. org/governance/beyond-afropessimism-historical-accounting-african-universities

Zolfagharifard, E. (2014, 04 February). Pictured: The 1,800-year-old face of 'Beachy Head Lady' is revealed for the first time thanks to 3D scanning. *The Daily Mail*. Retrieved from http://www.dailymail.co.uk/sciencetech/article-2551513/Pictured-The-1-800-year-old-face-Beachy-Head-Lady-revealed-time-thanks-3D-scanning

Chapter 2.

———〜〜〜———

Slavery and the Slave Trade: An Evolution

Slavery can be described as a form of human exploitation in which one human being is owned by another person. Historically, definitions of slavery have emphasised the legal status of the relationship; at a minimum, slavery gave a person legal rights over the movements and labour of another. In its more extreme form, however, the controls conferred by mastery extended over the body and personhood of the enslaved person. A slave thus hovered uncertainly between the contradictions of being both a piece of property and a person (Heuman & Burnard, 2011). Coercion could be used against slaves at will; their labour power, and even their sexuality, reproductive capacities, and gender were at the complete disposal of the master, such that enslaved parents could be separated from their children, men and women could be prevented from choosing their own mates and forced to accept those imposed by masters, and men and boys could be turned into eunuchs (Glancy, 2002; Heuman & Burnard, 2011).

Slavery is as old as human history. As early as 6800 BC, the Mesopotamians built strong external walls around their towns, suggesting a situation of ongoing raiding and warfare, and records from 2100 BC document the ownership of slaves by private citizens in Egypt (Heuman & Burnard, 2011). The word 'slave' is a Middle English version of the French word 'sclave', which itself derives from the Medieval and Late Latin 'sclāvus', a borrowing and Byzantine Greek σκλάβος *sklábos* 'slave' (Glancy, 2002). The word is believed to have originally meant literally 'Slav', as based on the fact that these peoples were often captured and forced into slavery in Central Europe during the early Middle Ages.

Slavery at its initial stage was not commercialised, and it was only much later that it became a business enterprise, yet the institution affected social and political structures from early times (Heuman & Burnard, 2011). The slave trade was an activity that transcended different cultures and countries; it was practised in China, India, Africa, the Americas and the Arab polities, among other regions. Slavery is frequently mentioned in the Bible, as Abraham and other personages owned servants, and of course, the Hebrews were themselves enslaved by the Egyptians. The Roman Empire also practised slavery, and according to Glancy (2002, p.9), 'slaves in the Roman Empire were vulnerable to physical control, coercion and abuse in settings as public as the auction block and as private as the bedroom'. During the Roman period, slaves had no inheritance or offspring, thus, they were automatically excluded from the cultural status of fatherhood.

Slavery in the British Empire

In ancient Britain, the institution of slavery dates at least to the Roman occupation. Anglo Saxons continued the process, often partnering with Vikings to make raids and sell slaves to the Irish, and Dublin was a major slave centre from the 9th to 12th centuries (Rodriguez, 1997). William the Conqueror allowed the enslavement of Britons to continue after 1066 but forbade their export to the slave markets of Europe (Loyn, 1991), and the Domesday Book census of 1086 indicates that over 10%

of England's population were slaves at that time (Davis, 1966). After the Norman Conquest, however, chattel slavery disappeared from practise, and the former slaves were merged into the serf population (Pelteret, 1995). Later, slave markets were established in Rome, Genoa, and Venice and expanded to other parts of the world. By the 13th century, slavery had become critical to the economy of Tuscany, fading only with Turkish control of the Eastern slave trade (Bales, 2005). The Catholic Church did not condemn the institution of slavery, though it decreed that Christians should not be sold.

The enslavement of British people took on a far different form in its colonies. From the 17th century, both major and petty crimes were punished by transport to the colonies in indentured servitude, and such sentences ranged from several years to life. Indentured servants either worked on projects for the colonial government or were forced to serve in households as labourers or domestic servants. The British colony of Australia began its history as a penal colony, and indentured servants in Britain's American and Caribbean colonies worked alongside and even sometimes lived with Blacks, who were themselves at first more often indentured. English and Irish indentured servants are recorded as having participated in rebellions against the colonial authorities in cooperation with Africans and Native Americans in colonies such as New York. It was not until the 18th century that the system of white servitude began to be formally separated from African slavery, although indentured servants were sent to the West Indies and Australia until the 1860s (Maxwell-Stewart & Oxley, 2017).

Slavery in Pre-Colonial African Societies

As in other regions around the world, the institution of slavery had been practised in Africa long before the Europeans started trading in African captives. No matter what window dressing we might try to impose on the term, ultimately, slavery involves the sale of individuals, and for African societies, slaves were seen as an emblem of status for both political and economic purposes. In African societies, slaves were usually war- or raid captives; most became servants and were eventually integrated into the household of their new masters. Moreover, slavery was not necessarily a permanent position in African societies. Historically, African slaves retained certain legal rights, and chattel slavery as practised in the Americas was unknown.

In pre-colonial African societies, slavery took on various forms, such as criminal slavery, which was an alternative punishment to death or maiming for certain infractions, or debt slavery, when an individual could not pay a creditor and was obliged to indenture himself/herself or a relative as a pawn to work off the repayment (Austin, 2017; Rodney, 1966). Pawnship was a common form of servitude practised among various groups in Ghana and Nigeria, such as the Igbo, Yoruba, Akan and the Ga (Lovejoy, 2012). Another form of slavery involved people who were suffering from famine or lived in fear of attack, who might place themselves or relatives in bondage to secure their nutrition or safety. Some slaves were kept as part of palace retinues or as the servants of other wealthy or noble personages (Rodney, 1966). In Uganda, Sudan, and parts of West Africa, a form of military slavery involving conscription was practised, whereby warlords would train and hire captives out or serve the patron's political interests (Lovejoy, 2012).

Slaves in domestic service were often incorporated into the master's lineage, and they retained some freedoms, such as the freedom to marry or earn independent monies. The children and other descendants of such slaves became closely intertwined with the family of the master, and many rose to prominent social positions. Olaudah Equiano reported that some slaves even owned slaves themselves (Equiano, 1790), and in larger states, a slave who showed exceptional skill or talent might be promoted to positions within the palace administration. The integration of war captives and other slaves into society was a serious and formal matter, and many societies, such as those of the Akan, had proverbs proscribing that their origins be forgotten.

The Atlantic Slave Trade (1400-1900)

The Trans-Atlantic slave trade was the largest forced migration in history. Before 1820, approximately four Africans arrived in the Americas for every European, and by the end of the 18th century, the number of African arrivals to the Americas had reached an estimated 8.7 million (Heuman & Burnard 2011). Overall, it has been estimated that the trans-Atlantic slave trade involved about 12-15 million Africans taken in forced migration, with about 10.6 million surviving the Middle Passage across the Atlantic (Table 2.1, Table 2.2).

Arab Muslims began trading in Black Africans from the eastern interior in the 7th century, exporting thousands of slaves annually to be sold throughout the Muslim world and further into Europe and across the Indian Ocean into Asia. When the Europeans took over the bulk of the trade in the 15th century, these numbers swelled into the millions. Ships travelling on outward-bound voyages of the Transatlantic slave trade started from home ports in Europe, packed with manufactured goods, before moving to the West African coast, where they were exchanged for slaves before moving into the Middle Passage across the Atlantic Ocean to the Americas. The Middle Passage was the most dangerous leg of the voyage, as ships were subjected to the buffeting effects of gales and storms, and the captives and crew often suffered from dehydration, malnutrition, or infectious diseases, which particularly affected the former, who were packed tightly below deck. Many of the newly enslaved chose not to endure the voyage, jumping overboard into the ocean, and the threat of uprisings was a constant concern. After several weeks of sailing, the ships would arrive at ports in the British 'sugar islands' of the Caribbean, the Spanish and Portuguese colonies of Central and South America, or the Chesapeake and southern colonies of North America, where the slaves were sold at auctions and plantation produce and goods such as sugar, tobacco, rice were packed into the ship for the return voyage to Europe.

Table 4. European participation in the Transatlantic Slave Trade

Country	Voyages	Slaves Transported
Portugal (including Brazil)	30,000	4,650,000
Spain (including Cuba)	4,000	1,600,000
France (including West Indies)	4,200	1,250,000
Holland	2,000	500,000
Britain	12,000	2,600,000
British North America, U.S.	1,500	300,000
Denmark	250	50,000
Other	250	50,000
Total	**54,200**	**11,000,000**

Table 5.[5] Number of slaves leaving African ports

Port	Number Departing	%
Senegambia (including Arguin), Sierra Leone	2,000,000	15.4
Windward Coast	250,000	1.9
Ivory Coast	250,000	1.9
Gold Coast (Ashanti)	1,500,000	11.5
Slave Coast (Dahomey, Adra, Oyo)	2,000,000	15.4
Benin to Calabar	2,000,000	15.4
Cameroons / Gabon	250,000	1.9
Loango	750,000	5.8
Congo / Angola	3,000,000	23.1
Mozambique / Madagascar	1,000,000	7.7
Total Leaving African Ports	13,000,000	100.0

At the initial stage of the expeditions, it was more difficult for the Europeans to obtain slaves, and they often had to sail long distances along rivers leading inland to find captives. After decades of European explorations, the Portuguese located the Gulf of Guinea in 1460 and a slave market was established in Lisbon. Over time, the Europeans had established a number of slave castles and 'factories' with the complicity of local chiefs and kings in or near various coasts along West and Central Africa (Dow, 1927).

Britain expanded the slave trade to an almost industrial scale to feed its need for labourers to work their plantations. It was said

---

[5] Source: http://www.slaverysite.com/Body/facts%20and%20figures.htm

that the English preferred African labour because they were better able to stand the rigours of tropical plantations compared to European labourers. Among notable early English traders were Sir John Hawkins and Sir Francis Drake, who acted on behalf of the British Navy to secure the Caribbean trade from Spanish control (Morgan, 2007). By the 16th century, the African slave trade had already brought thousands of Africans to Britain and its colonies. In 1562, Sir John Hawkins made three voyages to Sierra Leone and Guinea, where he violently kidnapped and transported a total of 1,200-1,400 enslaved Africans to the Caribbean colonies. In 1713, Britain was awarded the 'Asiento', which gave them the sole right to import an unlimited number of enslaved people to the Spanish Caribbean colonies for 30 years (Sorsby, 1975).

British Slavery and Colonialism in the Caribbean

The modern history of the Caribbean people dates to the voyages of Christopher Columbus, who arrived at the islands of Hispaniola, the Bahamas and Cuba in 1492 (Dunn & Kelley, 1989). At the time of the arrival of the Spanish, there were three major groups of indigenous peoples living on the islands. The Taínos, an Arawak speaking group were the dominant population in the Hispaniola, Puerto Rico, eastern Cuba, Jamaica, Trinidad, the Bahamas and the Leeward Islands, while the Caribs and Galibi occupied the Windward Islands and Trinidad and the Ciboney societies lived in western Cuba (Saunders, 2005).

The Spanish quickly subdued and enslaved the native populations of these islands, though some escaped into the mountains and forests. As the native peoples began dying from warfare, harsh labour the diseases brought by the Spanish, Africans began to be brought into the region to supplement them as a source of labour. As the Spanish

Empire began declining, other Europeans, namely the Portuguese, Dutch, the French and English, arrived to stake claims on the islands, and they also shipped in enslaved Africans to labour on the sugar plantations they established. Between the 16th century and the end of the 19th century, approximately four million Africans were brought over to the Caribbean islands from various parts of West and Central Africa (Martin, 2011).

A number of Africans escaped the Europeans and obtained refuge in the mountains among the remnants of the Tainos and Caribs (Aimes, 1967; Schroeder et al., 2018). The terrain of some islands ⏃such as Jamaica, Hispaniola, Cuba, Saint Vincent and Dominica⏃ included re-mote mountainous areas that were largely impenetrable by the Europeans, thus enabling many slaves to escape and form independent 'maroon' communities. Although most maroon communities were defeated as the Europeans began expanding their presence on the islands, these groups were especially tenacious in Haiti, as well as in Cuba, Puerto Rico and Jamaica, where maroon communities exist to this day. The maroon leader and *vodun* priest François Mackandal (d. 1758) led a widespread and devastating six-year rebellion against the French (Fick, 1990), and the predations of the Jamaican maroons endured from the 17th century until the mid-18th century, when the British were only able to end the warfare by promising them 2,500 acres of land in two locations and pay them a bounty for returning (rather than harbouring) other escaped African slaves (Campbell, 1988).

British laws governing slaves in the Caribbean were significantly stricter than French and Spanish law, which extended limited legal rights to slaves, such as the right to own property and enter contracts, and also recognised the ability of slaves to purchase their freedom (Rogozinsky, 2000). Under French law, such individuals who had purchased or been given their freedom gained full rights to citizenship (Rogozinsky, 2000). By contrast, British law prohibited the freeing of slaves without the consent of their master, and even freed slaves were never fully integrated into British colonial society, and could not own property, vote, or enter certain trades (Rogozinsky, 2000). However, while the British tended to maintain stronger legal and social separations between Europeans and Africans, overall, slave societies in the Caribbean were somewhat distinct from the system the British had established in the United States. One major factor in the difference was that people of African descent formed the majority population on the islands ⬚often up to 80%-90%, which made it more difficult for the Europeans to completely control the population or prohibit the continuation of African cultural practises.

Numerous violent uprisings broke out in the British Caribbean from the 17th to mid- 19th centuries, particularly in Jamaica (Rogozonski, 2000). On many of the islands, African customs were retained in cuisine, religion, naming practises and even some forms of language. For example, the religion of *vodun* (voodoo) practised in Haiti is directly traceable to the spiritual system of the same name practised among the Fon and Ewe speaking peoples of Benin, and southern and central Togo, and southern Ghana and Nigeria (Forte, 2010). In Jamaica, the leader of one of the most prolonged maroon wars was called 'Nanny', an Anglicised form of the title 'Nana' or 'Chief' among the Akan-speaking (Twi) peoples of Ghana, Ivory Coast and Togo, and among the extant Jamaican maroon communities is Accompong, which also directly derives from that language. Linguists have observed strong similarities between the creoles spoken by Jamaicans, Barbadians, and other African-Caribbean peoples and languages spoken in West Africa. For example, Jamaican patois is considered to be an English-based creole, yet it includes numerous loan words from West

African languages, particularly Akan, but also including Igbo and Yoruba (Cassidy, 1966; Cassidy & le Page, 2002; McWhorter, 2000).

By the 19th century, Britain was the dominant European power in the Caribbean, as the French had ceded many of its territories to England in the 17th and 18th centuries, and retained a hold over only Guadalupe, Martinique, Saint Martin, St. Barthelemy, Les Saintes and Marie-Galante following the Haitian Revolution (1791-1804). The Spanish had also ceded a number of its islands to Britain, and by the 19th century, their control extended only over Cuba, the eastern side of Hispaniola and Puerto Rico.

Following Britain's emancipation declaration in 1833, many Africans left the plantations, which created a severe work shortage on the sugar plantations. The British created an indentured labour scheme that closely resembled enslavement and first began bringing over workers from China, then later primarily from India and Southeast Asia (Tinker, 1993). The first ships carrying indentured Indian labourers for sugarcane plantations arrived in 1836, and over the 70-80 years, over half a million South Asians were brought to the Caribbean (Laurence, 1994; 'Indian Indentured Labourers', 2010). These Indo-Caribbean migrants now constitute a significant proportion of the population of many islands, including Trinidad and Tobago, Jamaica, British Guiana, French Guiana, Martinique, Guadalupe, and Grenada, among others. While some maintained their culture in separate communities, many blended with African-Caribbeans and other migrant-descendant communities to form a syncretic ethnic group. Their contribution to Caribbean culture is strongly evident in some elements of cuisine, such as curried meat dishes, *bhaji*, and rotis; however, some elements of Jamaican and other Caribbean creoles have also been traced to Hindi words (Cassidy & Le Page, 2002).

Slave Narratives and the Abolition Movement

One of the falsehoods spread about the Black people during the trans-Atlantic slave trade was that they were barbaric and had no intelligence; however, much like the exploits of such prominent Black figures as Harriet Tubman and Benjamin Banneker, the narrative experiences left by a few of these slaves has proven otherwise. The writings of some of these former slaves have been published in different volumes and used as historical sources as well as literary examples. Many of the authors of such narratives were also active in the ongoing effort to end slavery in Britain and its colonies. Africans who opposed slavery in the 18th century were often supported by White British in their efforts to end the institution. For example, Olaudah Equiano worked closely with Granville Sharp, a biblical scholar and abolitionist who developed the plan to settle freed Black people and poor Black people in England in Sierra Leone, as well as Thomas Clarkson, who campaigned worldwide for the end of slavery. As the MP for Yorkshire (1784-1812), William Wilberforce advocated for the abolition of the slave trade for twenty years until its abolishment with the enactment of the Slave Trade Act of 1807.

The slave experience was well documented by Olaudah Equiano (1790), a man from what is now Nigeria who became one of the greatest writers of his time. Equiano was born in an Igbo village named Essaka, where he was kidnapped at the age of 11 and eventually renamed Gustavas Vassa. As an adult, Equiano was able to buy his own freedom and went to England as a seaman in 1768. He eventually bea came an author, public speaker, and noted abolitionist. In 1789, Equiano published his autobiography in the form of an adventure story that became the prototype of the 19th-century slave narratives. Equiy ano's work has been recognised as being of great significance to African literature, and his narrative has been published in eight English editions as well as in other languages such as German and Russian.

Equiano advocated strongly against the evils of the slave trade, travelling all over Britain reading excerpts from his autobiography, lobbying in Parliament and mobilising public opinion. The Irish abolitionist Thomas Digges was highly impressed with Equiano and considered him as 'a principal instrument' in bringing about the motion for the passing of the Slave Trade Act of 1807 (Lovejoy, 2006).

Another advocate for emancipation was Quobna Ottobah Cugoano. Cugoano was born in 1757 in the Fanti area of the Gold Coast, where he was captured at the age of 13 and taken to Grenada as a slave before being purchased by an English merchant in 1772 and arriving in England, where his master sent him to school to learn to read and write (Edwards & Dabydeen, 1991). Later that year, he was freed as a consequence of the Somersett case, in which chattel slavery in England and Wales was declared to be unsupported by English common law.

As a free man, Cugoano joined Olaudah Equiano and others as an active member of the Sons of Africa, an abolitionist group whose members wrote frequent appeals to the newspapers of the day condemning the practise of slavery throughout the Empire. In 1787, he authored a passionate attack on the institution titled *Thoughts and Sentiments on the Evil and Wicked Traffic of the Slavery and Commerce of the Human Species*, in which he described the experiences of himself and others from the Gold Coast, argued for the immediate emancipation of all slaves, and declared that it was the duty of slaves to try to escape their bondage.

African-descended women also wrote slave narratives. Mary Prince was a Black woman originally born into a large family in Bermuda, though she and all of her siblings were eventually sold and dispersed all over the Caribbean. Mary was cruelly treated by her master and was forced to toil in the salt production industry in the Bahamas, which involved long working up to 17 hours standing in salt ponds, as a consequence of which her feet became deformed with boils that ate through her bones, causing her great torment (Prince, 1831). It was also documented that a part of her body was severely scarred from vestiges of severe floggings. Mary Prince was sold at different times to varying masters and at some point, left the West Indies for London in 1828 (Prince, 1831). Her floggings increased when she married Daniel James, a former Black slave who had purchased his freedom, and the free Black man began living with her on his property. Prince eventually escaped her master and worked with the anti-slavery society to campaign against the institution. Mary became the first woman to present an antislavery petition to the House of Parliament, as well as the first black woman to write an autobiography, which was titled 'The History of Mary Prince: A West Indian Slave'.

These examples demonstrate that the horrors, the slaves experienced did not stop them from aspiring to improve their status. Black people ascended from being packed like books upon an overflowing shelf aboard the slave ships to becoming authors and impassioned and eloquent advocates for freedom, thus marking an extraordinary transformation and achievement. People such as Equiano, Coguano, Prince and a host of others became abolitionists, public speakers, and left a legacy that others are still using as building stones today.

Contributions of Enslaved Africans to Britain and Europe

Africans made enormous contributions to the development and wealth of Britain and its colonies. Although this is not usually documented in literature, the Africans that were taken brought skills and knowledge along with their labour; however, these were rarely rewarded because the slave masters saw them as chattels. Some of the enslaved had been rulers in their homelands, and many had jobs as artisans, builders, farmers, fishermen, or hunters. Black people were also creative, and they brought their music and other arts with them to the lands to which they were taken.

Enslaved Blacks constructed buildings, laid the groundwork for cities, and fuelled the industries that made Britain and the other European countries the wealthy and powerful nations they are today. The slave trade stimulated major areas of commercial capitalism, such as shipbuilding, factories, banking, and insurance (Harley, 2013). African knowledge and skills in agriculture, blacksmithing, and medicine helped England's colonies to thrive, and slave labour produced the major consumer goods that became the basis of world trade, such as coffee, cotton, sugar, and tobacco. In British colonial areas such as the Carolinas, Virginia, and Maryland, iron and ironworking were major components of the economy. In the Chesapeake region of British North America, African metalworkers were first employed primarily in manual labour working with the raw materials but were gradually introduced to more skilled tasks as their advanced skills at the forge became impossible to ignore. By the mid-18th century, the Chesapeake alone was home to more than 60 ironworks, at which thousands of slaves assisted in or even supervised production, and by the American Revolutionary War, the British colonies in North America were producing about 30,000 tons of iron annually (Bezis-Selfa, 2004), making them the world's third-largest producer of iron (Lewis, 1974).

It is also little known that Colonial planters generally respected Africans' knowledge of herbs, medicines, and poison and that Africans contributed to cures of numerous diseases in Britain and its colonies based on their knowledge of similar diseases from the Old World. Africans are credited for bringing Europeans knowledge of birth by Caesarian section, inoculation methods for various infectious diseases, and cures for snake bites and other poisons (Holloway, 2015). Akans labouring in the Caribbean and the American South taught plantation owners medical techniques used to inoculate children with infectious matter from yaws, and throughout the colonies, they similarly performed smallpox variolations by simply taking some of the pus and inoculating those who had not yet been exposed (Holloway, 2015). Though previously, the mortality rate among Europeans had been nearly 100% for mothers on whom Caesarean sections were performed, survival rates improved dramatically after British travellers in the Buganda kingdom and other parts of the Great Lakes region during the 19th century observed the regular occurrence of successful Caesarean sections and studied African techniques ('Cesarean Section - A Brief History', 2013; Felkin, 1884).

Conclusion

This chapter has examined the history of slavery as it related to British and African interactions and development. It began with an overview of the institution of slavery, then reviewed slavery in precolonial Britain and African societies before engaging in a more extended discussion of the Transatlantic Slave Trade and its impacts on African and European economic and social development.

The Transatlantic Slave Trade had an enormously destructive impact on African societies and crippled economic and technological development on the continent. The displacement of over 12 million people, many of whom were knowledgeable in agriculture, medicine, metallurgy, and other technical areas left a drastic shortage of skills in the local industries. Moreover, the European powers engaged in on-going efforts to disrupt local social and political processes and foment conflict between the African polities, resulting in destabilisation and the free development of corrupt regimes. The devastation of villages, towns and societies through the slave trade and European-fostered wars left African states and societies severely underdeveloped and vulnerable to the predations of colonialism (Sherwood, 2007).

Following the scattering and settlement of Africans all over the world, the issue of the African diaspora emerged. People were not allowed bring their languages with them when they migrated; however, different voices emerged, many of which advocated for abolition and emancipation. Although Britain had abolished the slave trade in 1807, it did not emancipate the already enslaved Africans in its remaining Caribbean colonies until 1834, and this was followed by a four-to-six-year apprentice system, which ended in 1838 after massive resistance and protests from both Blacks and White abolitionists. Although emancipation put a halt to the forced importations of Africans to Britain, it ultimately stimulated pockets of voluntary migration. With the ending of slavery, British plantation owners and wealthy families were forced to seek other forms of inexpensive labour, and they began bringing Indian and Chinese labourers, some of whom ended up in England. Many emancipated slaves in the Caribbean joined the Merchant Navy and became seamen, and some ended up putting down roots in the small communities living in British port towns. Some of these migrants settled in the country and intermarried with native Whites. Towards the end of the 19th century, a number of African migrants travelled to England as students, and many of these individuals came to be instrumental in the struggle against colonial domination.

Thus, the latter half of the 19th century marked the beginning of the large-scale migration of Black and Asian people to Britain.

Additionally, during the 19th and 20th centuries, the British forcibly colonised parts of West Africa and opened up other forms of integration through the expansion of Christianity and the imposition of Western education, including the English language. The impact of this process can be seen in the number of Black Africans from former British colonies who have migrated to the UK and made it their home since the 1940s-1950s.

The next chapter continues our narrative of British and African interactions with a discussion of British colonial domination in Africa, the Pan-African movement, and how colonialism impacted African development and ultimately stimulated the opening of British borders to people of colour.

References

Aimes, H. H. S. (1967). *A history of slavery in Cuba, 1511 to 1868*. New York: Octagon Books.

Austin, G. (2017). Slavery in Africa, 1804-1936. In D. Eltis, S.L. Engerman, S. Drescher, & D. Richardson. *The Cambridge World History of Slavery: Volume 4, AD 1804–AD 2016* (pp. 174-196). New York: Cambridge University Press.

Bales, K. (2005). *Understanding global slavery: a reader*. Berkeley, CA: University of California Press

Bezis-Selfa, J. (2004). *Forging America: ironworkers, adventurers, and the industrious revolution*. Ithaca,NY: Cornell University Press.

Campbell, M.C. (1988), *The Maroons of Jamaica, 1655–1796: A History of resistance, collaboration & betrayal*. Granby, MA: Bergin & Garvey.

Cassidy, F.G. (1966). Multiple etymologies in Jamaican Creole. *American Speech*, 41(3),211-215.

Cassidy, F.G., & Le Page, R.B. (2002). A Dictionary of Jamaican English (2nd ed.). Kingston: University of the West Indies Press.

Cesarean Section - A Brief History. (2013). Bethesda, MD: U.S. National Library of Medicine. Retrieved from https://www.nlm.nih.gov/exhibition/cesarean/part2.html

Cugoano, O. & Cogoano, O. (1797). *Thoughts and sentiments on the evil and wicked traffic of the slavery and commerce of the human species: humbly submitted to the inhabitants of Great-Britain*. London, UK: Authors.

Davis, C.T., & Gates, H.L. (1985). *The slave's narrative*. Oxford, UK: Oxford University Press.

Davis, D. B. (1966). *The problem of slavery in western culture*. Oxford, UK: Oxford University Press.

Douglass, F. (1845). *Narrative of the life of Frederick Douglass, an American Slave*. Boston, MA: American Anti-Slavery Office

Dow, G.F. (1927). *Slave ships and slaving*. Salem, MA: Marine Research Society

Dunn, O., & Kelley, J.E. (trans.) (1989). *The diario of Christopher Columbus's first voyage to America, 1492-1493*. Norman and London: University of Oklahoma Press.

Edawards, P., & Dabydeen, D. (Eds.) (1991). *Black writers in Britain, 1760-1890*. Edinburgh: Edinburgh University Press

Equiano, O. (1790). *The interesting narrative of the life of Olaudah Equiano, or Gustavus Vassa, the African, written by himself*. London, UK: Author.

Felkin, R.W. (1884). Notes on labour in Central Africa. *Edinburgh Medical Journal*, 20, 922-930.

Fick, C. E. (1990). *The Making of Haiti: The Saint Domingue Revolution from below*. Knoxville: University of Tennessee Press.

Forte, J.R.A. (2010). Diaspora homecoming, vodun ancestry, and the ambiguities of transnational belongings in the Republic of Benin. In P. C. Hintzen, J.M. Rahier, & F. Smith (eds.), *Global circuits of blackness: interrogating the African diaspora*. Urbana-Champaign: University of Illinois Press.

Glancy, J.A. (2002). *Slavery in early Christianity*. Oxford, UK: Oxford University Press.

Harley, C.K. (2013). Slavery, the British Atlantic economy and the Industrial Revolution. Economics Series Working Papers Number 113, University of Oxford, Department of Economics. Retrieved from https://www.nuff.ox.ac.uk/Economics/History/Paper113/harley113.pdf

Heuman, G., & Burnard, T. (eds.) (2011). *The Routledge history of slavery*. London, UK: Routledge.

Holloway, J. (2015). Medicinal practises and folk medicine. In M.J. Shujaa & K.J. Shujaa (eds.), *The SAGE Encyclopedia of African Cultural Heritage in North America* (pp. 575-579). Thousand Oaks, CA: Sage.

Indian Indentured Labourers. (2010). The National Archives, Government of the United Kingdom.

Laurence, K. (1994). *A question of labour: indentured immigration into Trinidad and British Guiana, 1875-1917*. New York: St Martin's Press.

Lewis, R. L. (1974). Slavery on Chesapeake iron plantations before the American Revolution. *The Journal of Negro History*, 59(3), 242–254.

Lovejoy, P.E. (2006). Autobiography and memory: Gustavus Vassa, alias Olaudah Equiano, the African. *Slavery & Abolition: A Journal of Slave and Post-Slave Studies*, 27(3), 317-347. https://doi.org/10.1080/01440390601014302

Lovejoy, P.E. (2012). *Transformations of slavery: a history of slavery in Africa*. London: Cambridge University Press.

Martin, T. (2011). *Caribbean history: from pre-colonial origins to the present*. Boston: Pearson.

Maxwell-Stewart, H. & Oxley, D. (2017). Convicts and the colonisation of Australia, 1788-1868. Retrieved from https://www.digitalpanopticon.org/Convicts_and_the_Colonisation_of_Australia,_1788-1868

McWhorter, J. H. (2000). *The missing Spanish Creoles: recovering the birth of plantation contact languages*. Berkeley CA: University of California Press.

Morgan, K. (2007). *Slavery and the British Empire: From Africa to America*. Oxford, UK: Oxford University Press.

Prince, M. (1831). The *history of Mary Prince: a West Indian slave, related by herself*. London, UK: F. Westley and A. H. Davis.

Rodney, W. (1966). African slavery and other forms of social oppression on the Upper Guinea Coast in the context of the Atlantic slave-trade. *The Journal of African History*, 7(3), 431-443.

Rodriguez, J. (1997). *The historical encyclopedia of world slavery* (vol. 1). Ann Arbor: University of Michigan Press.

Rogozinski, J. (2000). *A brief history of the Caribbean*. London: Penguin.

Saunders, N. J. (2005). *The peoples of the Caribbean: an encyclopedia of archeology and traditional culture*. Santa Barbara, CA: ABC-CLIO.

Schroeder, H., Sikora, M., Gopalakrishnan, S., Cassidy, L.M., Delser, P.M., Velasco, M.S....& Willerslev, E. (2018). Genetic origins of the Caribbean Taino. *Proceedings of the National Academy of Sciences,* 115 (10), 2341-2346.

Sherwood, M. (2007). *British slavery and the trade in enslaved Africans*. London, UK: Institute of Historical research. Retrieved from http://www.history.ac.uk/ihr/Focus/Slavery/articles/sherwood.html

Smith, D.D. (1992). APA: *The ruin of a nation begins in the homes of its people*. Washington, DC: American Red Cross. Retrieved from https://resource.nlm.nih.gov/luna/servlet/detail/NLMNLM~1~1~101455760~159739

Sorsby, V.G. (1975) *British trade with Spanish America under the Asiento 1713-1740*. Doctoral thesis, University of London. Retrieved fromhttp://discovery.ucl.ac.uk/1349550/1/473433.pdf

Tinker, H. (1993). *New system of slavery*. London: Hansib Publishing.

Chapter 3.

———∾∾———

British Colonialism in Africa

In order to appreciate colonialism and its mechanisms of economic, political, and sociocultural control, we can begin by understanding the meaning of this term. Colonialism can be defined as the 'direct and overall domination of one country by another by state power being in the hands of a foreign power' (Ocheni & Nwanko, 2012). Among the main aims of colonialism is political domination, and once this is fully achieved, then the way is paved for further exploitation of the colonised country (Ocheni & Nwanko, 2012). As it operated in Africa between the period of 1900 and 1960, colonialism was an integral element of the broader phenomenon of imperialism, and one would exaggerate explaining colonialism as a direct form of imperialism (Ocheni & Nwanko, 2012).

In 1752, the Royal Trading Company was established to oversee Britain's trading interests in Africa, later to be replaced by the African Company of Merchants. Over the course of the 19th century, what are now the West African countries of Benin, Nigeria, Sierra Leone, Gambia, and Ghana became colonies of the then British Empire, while in East and Southern Africa, their control extended over Kenya, Uganda, Tanzania, Botswana, Lesotho, Zimbabwe, Namibia, Swaziland, Zambia, and parts of Sudan and Somalia.

The formal colonial relationship between Africa and Britain dates to the period between 1881 and 1914, when the European powers, most notably Portugal, Spain, Belgium, Italy, Germany, France and Britain scrambled and negotiated to achieve the division of the continent amongst themselves. However, the foundations of colonial rule can be directly linked to the tactics of control exercised from the time of the Transatlantic slave trade, when Europeans first built forts on the West African coast and began to subjugate Black Africans. Europe eventually took control of the African countries through ongoing diplomatic pressures and a series of military attacks.

One of the drivers of the scramble for the colonies was the difficulties faced by the rural areas of Britain in producing sufficient food to feed the fast-growing urban population. Britain's relationship with Africa during the Transatlantic slave trade had demonstrated that Africa had a ready market for such products, and the British focused on putting African labour to work on an industrial scale and seizing the raw materials of the African hinterland (Ocheni & Nwanko, 2012). Consequently, they directed the African economy in such a manner that suited the British economy.

The Spread of Christianity and Education in Africa

The spread of Christianity and Western cultural practises was another significant effect of colonialism. Christianity was introduced from Jerusalem to parts of Northeast Africa in the 1st to 2nd centuries AD in states such as Egypt, Eritrea and Ethiopia. However, the religion largely expanded into other parts of Africa through the work of European missionaries, beginning with the Portuguese in Central Africa in the 15th and 16th centuries, and continuing with French and British missionaries who spread along the coast and interior of West and East Africa in the 19th century.

Thus, although Christianity can be said to have entered colonised areas of Africa before the onset of formal colonialism, the missionaries were sponsored and protected by the European governments, and they are generally identified as a significant element in the entrenchment of European power in the area. Africans who converted to Christianity no longer remained under the full authority of traditional leaders, whose practises they had abjured, but rather allied themr selves to the missionaries and often helped to promote European interests in the area, as seen in the example of Samuel Ajayi Crowther in 19th century Nigeria. Christianity was often used to justify slavery and colonialism, such as with references to the curse of Ham, which places the origins of African enslavement in the Bible. Ham's son was made a slave to his brothers, as described in the quotation 'Cursed be Canaan, a slave of slaves shall he be to his brothers' (Genesis 9:25). From the Middle Ages, Africans were associated with these sons of Ham, as they were considered to have been 'blackened' by the weight of their sins, and this notion became increasingly intensified during the Transatlantic slave trade (Braude, 1997). Depictions of traditional African cultures and religions as barbaric also justified the imposition of Christianity, slavery, and colonialism, as advocates frequently expressed the belief that Africans needed Christianity and paternal domination to emerge from savagery into civilisation.

African Education during Colonialism

With the expansion of European imperialism, missionaries began introducing Western style university education. This was adopted early in settler colonies such as Sierra Leone, where the Fourah Bay College was established in 1826, as well as at Liberia College, which was founded in 1862. However, the colonial authorities were generally hesitant in encouraging higher education for Black African students, and even after colonisation, there were some cherry-picking in respect to where higher educational institutions were established. It was feared that access to Western education might inspire modernised African elites would seek to demand more equal rights and shares, which the colonial authorities feared would lead to further competition and rivalry. Nonetheless, over time, other higher institutions were established across Africa, with the exception of Belgian and Portuguese Africa, where harsher, more servile forms of colonial dominance were imposed. Most of the British colonial university colleges served as regional universities but were affiliated with and awarded degrees from the University of London (Table 4.2).

Table 6. List of African universities founded by British colonial authorities (Zeleza, 2006).

Fourah Bay College: Founded in Sierra Leone in 1826.
Liberia College: Founded in 1862.
Gordon Memorial College: Founded in the Sudan in 1902; renamed Khartoum University College in 1951 and then as Khartoum University at Independence in 1956.
The Islamic Institute: Founded in the Sudan in 1912; it became a college in 1924 and was renamed the Omdurman Islamic University in 1965.
Cairo University: Founded in Egypt in 1908 despite the vehement opposition of the colonial governor. It grew to become one of the largest universities in Africa, with a student population of 155,000 students and more than 5,500 faculty members and instructors. In 1938 the university formed a branch in Alexandria, which later became Alexandria University in 1942.
Inter-State Native College: Established in South Africa in 1916 and later renamed the University College of Fort Hare in 1951. The institution produced Fort Hare a list of alumni includes such nationalist leaders as Nelson Mandela, Seretse Khama, and Robert Mugabe.
Makerere Government College: Established in Uganda in 1921. It began as a vocational school before it was turned into Makerere University College in 1949.

Yaba Higher College: Established in Nigeria in 1932 and served for years as the country's major higher education institution.

Government Training College: Founded in Ghana in 1927. Later renamed the Prince of Wales School and College, Achimota, among its most famous instructors was Dr. Kwegyir Aggrey, the eminent educator, and prominent alumni include Kwame Nkrumah, who obtained his teacher's certificate there in 1930. These colleges were often affiliated with and provided courses, examinations, and qualifications from British universities.

University Colleges in Nigeria: Founded in Ibadan, Nigeria in 1947.

University College: Established in Ghana in 1948.

University College: Established in Sudan in 1949 following the merger of the Gordon Memorial College and the Kitchener Medical School.

Royal Technical College: Established in Nairobi, Kenya in 1951.

University College of Salisbury: Founded in Zimbabwe in 1953 and renamed two years later as the University College of Rhodesia and Nyasaland.

Sierra Leone: Britain's First African Colony

By the end of the 15th century, the Portuguese—who had been welcomed by local leaders—had built a fort on the coast in Sierra Leone, where they were soon joined by Dutch and French traders. These Europeans used Sierra Leone as an early base from which to purchase slaves from African traders travelling from the interior. However, by the 17th century, the British had come to dominate European trade in the area, and around 1628, they established a trading post near Sherbro Island, about 50 km south-east of present-day Freetown (Fyfe, 1962). In 1663, a company called the Royal Adventurers of England Trading into Africa (later renamed the Royal African Company of England) obtained a charter from the Crown and constructed a fort on Tasso Island in the Freetown estuary, although continuous plundering by Dutch and French operators eventually led to the relocation of that fort to nearby Bunce Island (Fyfe, 1962). Throughout this period until later in the 18th century, the British relied on Afro-Portuguese as their intermediaries with the local rulers; however, these middlemen often tended to side with the local communities against the British traders, such as in 1728, when they joined together to destroy the Bunce Island fort (Fyfe, 1962).

In 1787, the Crown founded a settlement at Freetown with the intention of using it as a place to re-settle Black Americans whom the Empire had freed in return for their loyalty during the American Revolutionary War, many of whom were languishing among the 'Black Poor of London', which also included small populations of Africans and West Indians. The initial group of 400 Blacks and 60 English tradesmen were established in the 'Province of Freedom', also called Granville Town (named after British abolitionist Granville Sharp, who had organised the mission); however, most of the settlers soon died due to illness and attacks from the nearby Mende and Temne communities. A second, equally unsuccessful Granville Town was built near Fourah Bay (Walker, 1992). In 1792, a successful colony was established when nearly 1200 Black people from the Canadian province of Nova Scotia, who had been British Loyalists during the American Revolution, arrived and built Freetown on the former site of the first Granville Town. These former American slaves established lives largely modelled after those they had led in the American South, including styles of architecture, dress and speech and the continued practise of the Methodist religion (Walker, 1992). Although they attempted to take control of the land from the British as freeholders, the Crown countered such efforts, even bringing in 500 Jamaican Maroons to subdue a Black settler revolt in 1799 (Walker, 1992).

In the first decades of the 19th century, Sierra Leone was at the centre of British efforts to end the slave trade and 'rehabilitate' West Africa after centuries of slave trading. The British colony at Sierra Leone served as the headquarters for the interception of slave ships in the first thirty years after the abolition of the slave trade, and thousands of liberated captives were settled in the colony. Whereas some have considered this action to have been an exercise in British abolitionism, others have termed these later settlers as 'recaptives', as in fact, most were either forced to join the British Navy or sold as 'apprentices' to the White settlers, the Black Nova Scotian settlers, and the Jamaican Maroons (Schwartz, 2012). The apprentice system had many qualities analogous to slavery, and the 'liberated' captives were often unpaid and abused by the settlers. Many were forced to assimilate into Western cultures by taking on new names and adopting Christian practises, and some risked being sold back into slavery by escaping the colony and returning to their home villages or joining native settlements (Schwartz, 2013). For example, in June 1808, a group of 21 men and women ran away to the nearby native settlement of Robiss, yet they were soon recaptured and imprisoned by the settlers (Schwartz, 2012).

Over time, many of the liberated West African captives did settle into their lives in Freetown, and over the 19th century, they mingled with the West Indians, freed African Americans, and refugees from the newly established American colony of Liberia who also immigrated and settled in the area (Walker, 1992). Together, these disparate groups of African descent created a new creole ethnicity and trading language, both of which came to be called Krio (Lewis, 2009). The Krios acted as intermediaries between the British and the indigenous peoples of the interior, and many gained higher statuses through their positions in the colonial government. Today, the Krio language is the most widely used in the country.

In the early-mid 19th century, Freetown served as the centre of British colonial administration in West Africa, and it also became an educational centre after the establishment of Fourah Bay College in 1827. For over a century, this was the only European-style university in West Africa, and it drew English speaking Africans from across the region. By the end of the 19th century, however, British hegemony had spread throughout West Africa. In 1896, Britain annexed the inland areas adjacent to Freetown a to form the Sierra Leone Protectorate, and as the colonial government became more entrenched in the area, they began recruiting British officers, pushing the Krios out of their administrative positions and the upper-status neighbourhoods that they had established in Freetown (Harris, 2012).

Colonialism and the Pan-African Movement

The concept of Pan- Africanism was born out of the need to address racism and colonialism. To achieve this, it was considered imperative that all peoples of African descent be organised and united. Pan Africanism can be defined as including those of African descent 'whose lives and work have been concerned, in some way, with the social and political emancipation of African peoples and those of the African diaspora. What underlies their manifold visions and approaches is the belief in some form of unity or common purpose among the peoples of Africa and the African diaspora' (Adi, 2003).

As European colonial activity in Africa continued unabated, leading to the scramble for Africa and the onset of the era of imperialism, the crimes perpetrated against those of African descent were excused and justified by racist ideologies. Thus, during this period, a struggle emerged to 'vindicate the race' and refute notions of African inferiority, and some of these activists became pioneers in the development of pan-African thinking (Adi 2003).

Many of the most notable efforts in initiating change among the status of the Black people have been attributed to African and Caribbean students, who had begun to organise themselves by the late 19th century to promote the interests of their countries of origin, forge unity with each other, and combat the effects of discrimination in Britain. Dissatisfaction with colonial rule and racism led many West African students to seek radical solutions, and they met with British anti-colonial forces such as the League of Imperialism. These students were able to exert significant pressure in furthering what they saw as West Africa's (and therefore their own) political and economic future.

Following several failed attempts to form African political organisations, the African Association was established in London under the leadership of the Trinidadian barrister Henry Sylvester Williams in 1897. A Sierra Leonean law student named T.J. Thompson became the group's vice chairman, and a Nigerian medical student at Edinburgh University, Moses Da Rocha, served as its executive. The Association was formed to encourage a feeling of unity and facilitate friendly interactions among African descended people in general. Their larger goal was to support and defend the interests of all subjects claiming African descent in the British Colonies by circulating accurate information on the issues affecting their rights and privileges as subjects of the British Empire and by making direct appeals to the imperial and local governments.

Three years after the formation of the African Association, another meeting led by Williams was convened in London and attended by 37 delegates and about ten other participants from Africa, the UK, the Caribbean and the United States, including the famous Pan-African activist W.E.B. DuBois, John Archer and Henry Francis Downing. The aim of the movement was to solve the problem of the colour line, which they saw as the definitive issue of the 20th century, and to secure civil and political rights for Africans and their descendants throughout the world, particularly through liberation from the colonial activities of the imperialist powers in Africa, the Caribbean and elsewhere (Adi & Sherwood, 2003). Students were highly active in this movement, and the outcome of their political activities saw the birthing of a Pan-African political milieu in Britain. Throughout the twentieth century, West African and Caribbean students made strong contributions to this cause through the Pan-African organisations, whose members often met to discuss matters of vital significance concerning Africa and the Negro race. The students sought to raise the status of African people and extol the virtues of a glorious African past, and they contested racism and the colour bar in Britain. As Bandele Omoniyi, a Nigerian from Lagos studying in Edinburgh, raged, 'the treatment accorded to Africans in the Native land and abroad by the ignorant classes of white men and those who ought to know better generally makes one's blood boil' (Osborne & Kent, 2015, p. 120). Before 1945, many of the leading political figures in Pan-African history lived and worked in the diaspora rather than in Africa, and for a time, Britain was a centre of the Pan-African world. Of the seven Pan-African Congresses held between 1900 and 1994, four were held in Britain, namely in London (1900, 1921, 1923) and Manchester (1945).

Outside of Britain, quite a few leaders were instrumental in the fight for the establishment of Pan-Africanism, including William E. Du Bois and Marcus Garvey (born in Jamaica). Garvey became one of the most famous advocates of Pan-Africanism, establishing a movement called the Universal Negro Improvement Association (UNIA), which had its headquarters based in New York and boasted millions of supporters throughout Africa and the diaspora. Garvey's slogans asserted 'Race first' and 'Africa for the Africans at home and abroad'. W.E.B Du Bois, an attendee at the first Pan-African Conference in London in 1900 and an activist for Black rights in the United States, organised a series of Pan-African Congress meetings. Other famous Pan-Africanists were the Trinidadian journalist George Padmore, the American scholar Alphaeus Hunton, and Nigerian activists Chief Obafemi Awolowo and Prince Jaja Wachuku (Adi & Sherwood 2003). A major contributor to Pan-Africanism from West Africa was Kwame Nkrumah; whose achievements included an instrumental role in bringing an end to British colonial rule in the Gold Coast and leading Ghana's transition to independence in 1957. Many Africans in the diaspora moved to Ghana, and a new type of Pan-Africanism was formed that centred on the African continent and ultimately led to the founding of the Organisation of African Unity (OAU) in 1963. The efforts of the Pan-Africanists contributed to the end of colonialism throughout most of Africa over the course of the 1960s, though it was not until the end of apartheid in South Africa in 1991 that the entire continent was liberated from the grip of European colonialism.

African Contributions to British Military Efforts

Opportunities for social advancement were extremely limited for Africans living under slavery and colonialism. Unwilling to face continued work under the harsh positions of Caribbean plantations or feeling constrained by the lack of access to positions within the colonial administrations in Africa, many Black people living in the British colonies chose to depart their homelands, and some succeeded in obtaining positions as servants in wealthy households in England or elsewhere in the empire. However, the bulk of migrants found their escape through joining the British armed forces, and people of African descent made numerous contributions to British military efforts in the late 19th and early-to-mid 20th centuries. Many slaves in North America received their freedom in exchange for supporting the British armies as labourers or skilled workers and spies during the American Revolution, and some even fought as part of the 'Ethiopian Regiment' led by Lord Dunmore, the royal governor of Virginia (Lanning, 2000). A number of liberated African captives of Sierra Leone joined the British Navy, such as the surgeon, soldier and political activist James Africanus Horton, (1835-1883). Other formerly enslaved Black people from the Caribbean and Africa, also joined military service, such as Olaudah Equiano, who became a merchant seaman soon after purchasing his freedom in 1768. An African born in the Sudan named James Durham also served in the military services in the 18th century. After the British Empire's Emancipation Proclamation in 1834, a number of African-Caribbean men became seamen in the Merchant Marines as a means of escaping plantation labour, and the wages they earned allowed them to support their families, purchase properties, and establish businesses back home upon their retirement (Cobley, 2004). In addition, at least one woman of African-Caribbean descent, British-Jamaican business woman and nurse Mary Seacole (1805-1881), also aided British military efforts, setting up the British Hotel during the Crimean war (1853-1856), where she cared for wounded soldiers on the battlefield.

When World War I broke out in 1914, many of these merchant marines joined the British war effort, travelling from the Caribbean at their own expense to fight against the Germans. Over 15,000 West Indian men served as soldiers in the British West Indies Regiment (BWIR) of the British Army (Bourne, 2014). These soldiers performed dangerous tasks such as loading ammunition, laying telephone wires and digging trenches; however, they were not permitted to fight. By the end of the war, nearly 1300 of them had died from injuries or illness, and 697 had been wounded. Among the names of African-Caribbean men who served in the war is Sergeant William Gordon, a Jamaican who served in the army forces, and the Guyanese merchant seaman Lionel Turpin, who was just 19 years old when he enlisted in the British Army and earned two medals in the battles of the Somme (Bourne, 2014). Among the most celebrated of the Black Caribbean soldiers in WWI was Lieutenant Walter Daniel John Tull (28 April 1888 – 25 March 1918), the son of a Black man from Barbados and an English mother, who enlisted in the British Army in 2014 and lost his life during the First Battle of Bapaume in northern France (Bourne, 2015).

Other Black soldiers were recruited from British colonies in Africa, particularly Nigeria, the Gold Coast, Sierra Leone, Gambia and South Africa to defend their countries borders from German incursions. Throughout the First World War, approximately 120,000 West and East Africans served in uniformed Labour Units of various branches of the British armed forces, along with some 60,000 Black South Africans (Bourne, 2014).

Black involvement in British military efforts increased significantly during the Second World War, as Africans in British colonies worldwide became engulfed in the struggle against the Axis powers. Britain began making frequent appeals to the colonies for aid in the early years of the war, and numerous Africans and Black Caribbeans joined the war effort as field workers, merchant seamen, and servicemen from the army, navy, and air forces. Overall, tens of thousands of Black Caribbeans enlisted in the British armed forces; however, the numbers of African soldiers and field workers from the British colonies reached nearly three-quarters of a million, with 200,000 soldiers recruited under the West Africa Command, over 320,000 men from

British East Africa, and additional 136,000 from South Africa. Some of these soldiers and workers ended up stationed in Britain, and many settled there after the war. For example, 345 West Indians came to work in munitions factories in and around Liverpool in 1941 (Wilson, 1998). By the end of the war, approximately 10,000 Black people had settled in small communities concentrated in the dock areas of London, Liverpool and Cardiff. As described in Chapter 5, similar needs for labour and assistance drove the government's recruitment of Caribbeans, and later Africans and Asians, in the late 1940s-early 1950s, which resulted in much larger influxes of Black people to England and formed the foundation of Black British society as we know it today.

Conclusion. The Impact of Colonialism on Africa

This chapter has examined the history and lasting impacts of British and European colonialism in Africa, as well as contributions of Africa to British society, security, and economic growth, and finally considered obstacles to and expanding areas of African development. Colonialism completed the work of slavery by destroying indigenous African social and political structures. The division of Africa between the European powers at the Berlin Conference in 1885 ignored previous historical boundaries, language groups and kingdoms, and colonial administrators often deliberately restructured local political structures to facilitate their ability to control local populations.

Colonialism also resulted in the destruction of much indigenous manufacturing in Africa, such as iron production, which had reached industrial levels before the markets were flooded with cheaper metal products imported from Europe. Africa's role in the world economy as a supply of raw materials for major consumer manufactured products can be traced back to the period of colonial dominance and exploitation. Today, that cycle continues, although many African states (countries) might not recognise or acknowledge this. Even though African countries fought for their independence, they have struggled to transfer sovereignty to areas of economic growth, and largely depend on aid from China and Western nations to deal with debts and bolster their failing infrastructures.

Colonialism involved the spread of racist ideology to justify the enslavement and subjugation of Africans. Along with socio-political disruptions and economic underdevelopment, racist ideology has left Africans with a massive 'existence insecurity' that connotes a 'persistent generalised sense of threat and unease, because their survival is systematically threatened on every level-personal, family, community, culturally and nationally' (Norris & Inglehart, 2004). Martha Cabrera (2002), a Nicaraguan psychologist, has argued that 'populations that are wounded as a product of permanent stress lose their capacity to make decisions and plan for the future due to the excess suffering they have lived through and not processed'. In slightly diluted forms, racism remains with us today, perhaps most perniciously in the distortions of African history in many school curricula (Sherwood, 2007).

Even as we cannot ignore the devastating impact of slavery and colonialism on Africa's development, we must also recognise the ways in which its participation in these atrocities have fuelled Britain's own economic prosperity, and we must acknowledge the enormous contributions of Africans and Caribbeans to British society. Britain's colonies in Africa and the Caribbean were sources of enormous wealth in the form of raw materials and labour, which fuelled the country's economic growth, and the Black people in these colonies also contributed to the nation's security through their massive participation in war efforts. Many of these individuals (particularly from the Caribbean) eventually migrated to Britain, building small communities or joining the groups of Black British already settled in the country and bringing their music, cuisines, and other cultural elements that have infused British social life. After the Second World War, these communities would form a core around which later influxes of Black Caribbean and African migrants would grow to be firmly entrenched as members of Black British society.

References

Adi, H., & Sherwood, M. (2003). *Pan-African history: political figures from Africa and the Diaspora since 1787*. London, UK: Routledge

Braude, B. (1997). The sons of Noah and the construction of ethnic and geographical identities in the medieval and early modern periods. *William and Mary Quarterly* 54(1), 103-192.

Cabrera, M. (2002). Living and surviving in a multiply wounded country. *Revista Envío*, 257. Retrieved from http://www.envio.org.ni/articulo/1629

Fyfe, C. (1962). *A history of Sierra Leone* (vol. 1). Oxford: Oxford University Press.

Fyle, C.M. (2015, 22 June). Pedro da Çintra did not name Sierra Leone: an exploration into available evidence. *Concord Times*. Retrieved from -http://sl-concordtimes.com/pedro-da-cintra-did-not-name-sierra-leone-an-exploration-into-available-evidence/

Harris, D. (2012). *Civil war and democracy in West Africa: conflict resolution, elections and justice in Sierra Leone and Liberia*. London: I.B. Tauris.

Kaplan, I. (1976). *Area handbook for Sierra Leone*. Washington, D.C.: U.S. Government Printing Office.

Kup, A.P. (1961). *A history of Sierra Leone, 1400-1787*. Cambridge: Cambridge University Press.

Lewis, M. P. (Ed.) (2009). *Ethnologue: languages of the world* (16 ed.). Dallas, Texas: SIL International.

Norris, P., & Inglehart, R. (2004). *Sacred and secular – religion and politics worldwide*. New York, NY: Cambridge University Press

Ocheni, S., & Nwanko, B.C. (2012). Analysis of colonialism and its impact in Africa. *Cross-Cultural Communication*,8(3), 46-54.

Osborne, M., & Kent, S.K. (2015). *Africans and Britons in the age of empires*, 1660-1980. London, UK: Routledge.

Schwartz, S. (2012). Reconstructing the life histories of liberated Africans: Sierra Leone in the early nineteenth century. *History in Africa*, 39, 175-207.

Schwartz, S. (2013). Reconstructing the life histories of enslaved africans: Sierra Leone, c. 1808-19. Paper presented at the 127th Annual Meeting American Historical Association, New Orleans, LA, January 3-6, 2013.

Walker, J. W (1992). *The Black Loyalists: The search for a promised land in Nova Scotia and Sierra Leone, 1783-1870*. Toronto: University of Toronto Press.

PART 2

Purpose

These chapters from the volume 'Globalisation, human security and social inclusion' provide a detailed discussion of patterns of modern African migrations to Britain, issues impacting African social and economic development and the evolution of British immigration policies regarding Africans.

Method/Approach

This study is informed by the use of primary and secondary sources, including UK government documents and compiled statistics regarding migration and related policies, as well as newspaper articles, sociological reports and analyses, and social, economic and demographic statistics published by international organisations such as the United Nations and the World Bank. The author also includes several case studies based on interviews with migrants.

Findings

This study demonstrates that issues limiting African socio-economic development have played a large role in stimulating African migration to the UK; however, such migration has exacerbated these problems by causing a brain drain from African to more developed countries.

Many cases of African and African Caribbean migrations to the UK have been initiated by Britain, which has benefitted by recruiting migrants for lower-wage jobs. Despite the clear economic benefits sought from and conferred by the presence of immigrants, many White Britons have actively resisted the presence of darker-skinned peoples, and the government has enabled xenophobic sentiments by imposing increasingly restrictive measures aimed at curbing immigration from Africa and the Caribbean.

Originality/Value

This study firmly punctures some prevailing myths about Black immigration to the UK by demonstrating that 'Black minority ethnic' migrants in fact have a history of contributions to British economic development at the expense of their own native countries; however, the government's labour needs have conflicted with social conceptualisations of nationality and security.

Chapter 4.

――᷾――

African Migration and Development

There are a variety of circumstances that cause people to migrate. On the positive side, some move because they were offered jobs in one of the developed countries, others because they have an exisiting support network. For example, it is possible for a migrant to already have generations of family already living in the UK, and others move because they found love and want to join their partners/spouses. However, negative circumstances have continued to push many young people and professionals out of Africa to all other countries, all over the world. It has been suggested that Africa loses about £192bn to the rest of the world every year, while only £134bn flows in. Thus, the impacts of severe limitations on sustained growth are among the primary push factors for migration in many African states. At the basic level of infrastructure, it has led to lack of quality healthcare and services for those with physical and intellectual disabilities, as well as food insecurity, rising unemployment, poverty, and heightened vulnerabilty to natural disasters, climate change, and famine. At the socio-cultural level, we have seen the stigmatisation of those with mental illness, HIV, or disabilities, gender and income inequality, increased violence against women, the rise of ethnic and religious conflict,a nd a lower respect for the value of life. At the political level, causes and results of limited growth include corruption and graft, as well as national insecurity due to internal conflicts and the rise of extremist groups.

With many of the developed countries closing their doors on immigration, it has become imperative for African countries to examine ways of creating enabling environments for their citizens and incentives for those in the diaspora to return home. Unfortunately, even after several decades of independence, many African countries have not achieved the necessary economic growth and development to put them on the same level as other developing countries. Many African nationalists, scholars, and other progressive thinkers have attributed the inconsistent slow growth in certain sectors in some African countries to external causes, namely continued 'neo-colonial' interference from Western countries and the proliferation of activity by multi-national corporations exploiting Africa's labour and natural resources. Some African scholars have even advocated the abandonment of alien political structures introduced by colonialists in favour of a return to traditional values. However, playing this 'blame game' without proffering sustainable solutions is a waste of time, and it is utterly useless in considering the problem of massive migration and Africa's 'brain drain'.

The attraction of better job opportunities has continued to pull many graduates away from Africa. It is not uncommon for prospective immigrants to flock to various foreign embassies to obtain visas for any of the developed country that would admit them. On the other hand, it is the desire of these developed nations such as the UK, US and Canada to attract highly skilled professionals, thus resulting in a brain gain for these countries, and a brain drain for the sending countries. Brain drain is not a new phenomenon; some have argued that the brain drain for Africa began with the removal of millions of talented individuals during the Arab and trans-Atlantic slave trades. In modern times, it began in small scales of migration in the 1960s and became very pronounced in many African states in the 1980s during periods of economic recession.

It is estimated that about 150,000 expatriate professionals are employed in various African countries at about USD$4 billion a year. The downside of this migration drain is that African countries receive little return for their investment because the migrants who move to developed counties such as the UK rarely return to their home countries, and those who do return primarily do so due to challenges in their adopted lands such as personal insecurity, fraud, or lack of medical facilities to look after them and their families. The implications of this is that whenever there are medical emergencies or any other gap that requires human resources, Africans mostly employ foreigners from abroad (who are usually not Africans) to address the problem. There are many Africans who fervently wish to contribute to the continent's development; however, state governments have made this difficult by not providing a sustainable environment for them to work and live.

Many African states witnessed declining growth in commodity export volumes and prices from the late 1970s to the 1990s, which resulted in massive business failures and proliferating unemployment, which in turn fuelled a brain drain in many African countries, particularly among health care professionals (Busse, Erdogan & Muhlen, 2014). In order to revitalise African economies, international financial institutions such as the International Monetary Fund (IMF) and the World Bank imposed strict SAPs(Structural Adjustment Programmes), which diverted funds from development as governments scrambled to meet the imposed terms. Of course, SAPs created more problems for Afriɾ ca's fragile economy due to conditional lending systems that many states found unsustainable, and a number of analysts have attributed the continuing dependency and poverty of many developing nations to such policies (Shah, 2013). Africa's growth has long been subservis ent to external powers such as the global economy and the Western world, however, most states in Africa have little to show for this in terms of economic development and good governance.

Other analysts have identified the absence of popular democracy as a major cause for Africa's crisis of development since the 1970s (Offor, 2006). African countries have witnessed profound governance chang es since the beginning of the 1990s (Bratton & Van De Walle, 1997). Many states have moved from military rule to democracy, however, sustaining these relative freedoms is challenging. Although some sece tors have shown considerable improvement, economic development has remained static or slow in many African states, and security chal lenges such as political oppression, mismanagement of public funds, corruption, violent conflicts, and ecological deterioration have disu couraged investors and slowed economic growth.

Since the 1960s, Africa's share of world trade has fallen to only about 2%, and more than 40% of the continent's one billion people live below the internationally recognised poverty line of USD$1 a day. Meanwhile, the continent's population is undergoing unprec edented and sustained growth, and is expected to double by 2050. Many people lack decent health status, education, access to basic infrastructure, and other resources needed to benefit from and contribute to economic growth. Approximately 40% of Africans live in rural areas. An estimated 590 million African people (57% of the population) have no access to electricity and 700 million (68% of the population) lack clean cooking facilities (UN Department of Economic and Social Affairs, 2018). If these current energy access trends continue, then in 2030, there will still be 655 million people in Africa (42% of the population) without access to power, and 866 million (56% of the population) without clean cooking facilities, thus depriving the majority of the population of the opportunity to pursue a healthy and productive life (UN Department of Economic and Social Affairs, 2018).

Africa's Development Dynamics

Despite these challenges, there are areas of growth and development that deserve mentioning. According to the World Bank, economic growth in Africa continues to experience a steady recovery. As of 2018, the growth forecast for African economies was 3.1%, marking a significant increase from 2.4% in 2017, and a further increase of 3.6% is projected in 2019-2020 (Kambou, 2018). Most of 2018's top performers are non-commodity intensive economies. The list is led by Ghana (8.3%), which is boosted by oil & gas expansion, Ethiopia (8.2%), Côte d'Ivoire (7.2%), Djibouti (7%), Senegal (6.9%) and Tanzania (6.8%) (Kambou, 2018). Africa is currently home to six of the world's ten fastest growing economies (Adegoke, 2018).

Renewable Energy-solar energy

One rapidly expanding sector in Africa is renewable energy technology (RET). The continent is blessed with substantial renewable energy resources, many of which remain underexploited. It is predicted that if enough entrepreneurs can engage in commerce related to solar energy, a trillion-dollar market could be generated for Africa. The impact of such growth would be more jobs for the unemployed, which would in turn reduce the need for migrants to leave the continent in search of jobs. Moreover, investment in renewable energy would enhance the sustainability of economic development and help contribute to cleaner energy goals.

Agriculture

The agricultural sector is critical to many of Africa's greatest development goals. It has been suggested that farming alone accounts for 60% of total employment in Sub-Saharan Africa. According to a World Bank report, agriculture accounts for 32% of Gross Domestic Product (GDP), employs 65% of the labour force, and contributes over 80% of trade in value and more than 50% of raw materials to industries (Kambou, 2018). However, this aspect of growth is often ignored by university graduates, as farming and agriculture has usually been conducted by uneducated people living in rural communities. Analysts believe that if agriculture can be infused with up-to-date technology, it will become a more attractive industry to younger, more educated Africans, thus helping to reduce poverty and improve food security goals.

Tourism

The tourism industry has long been a flourishing business in Africa, providing employment for millions of people on the continent. In 2012, Africa received about $36 billion in receipts from tourism, which represents an increase of 2.8 % compared to the previous decade (World Bank, 2013). If growth in this sector continues at current rates, then by 2026, African tourism's contribution to Gross Domestic Product (GDP) will amount to $296 billion. This estimate includes tourism from within the continent, which currently exceeds visitors from Western nations (World Bank, 2013). Africa has expansive landscapes and formidable animal life that captivate visitors, as does the friendliness of Africans towards foreign visitors in their midst. Nonetheless, although tourism injects money into local economies, it also has its pitfalls. Some countries do not welcome Western tourists and accuse them of disrespecting their culture. For example, Islamic fundamentalists in Egypt, who are incited by tourist behaviours that conflict with their own cultural codes, have waged a terrorist campaign against foreign visitors with disastrous results for that country's tourism industry. Interethnic conflicts, religious clashes, and publicised crimes against international tourists also have impacted the financial benefits from tourism.

Africa's Creative Economies

The United Nations Conference on Trade and Development's Creative Economy Report 2008 defined the creative economy as encompassing the interface between creativity, culture, economics and technology as expressed in the ability to create and circulate intellectual capital, with the potential to generate income, jobs and export earnings while at the same time promoting social inclusion, cultural diversity and human development. This is what the emerging creative economy has already begun to do.

Many analysts believe that Africa has the potential to build a sustainable economy through promoting its own heritage. There is growing international interest in the ability of Africa's cultural and creative industries to drive sustainable development and create inclusive job opportunities. The cultural and creative industries in Africa generate an estimated USD $4.2 billion and 547,500 jobs annually through the informal economy (Bekenova, 2016). Digital distribution in industries such as design, films and music has transformed global markets and allowed new industries and consumers to emerge in developing regions (OECD-2, 2005). The Nigerian Nollywood film industry alone generates USD $500 million - $800 million annually and is estimated to directly employ some 300,000 people ('Africa & Middle East: A Rising CCI Market', 2018). In recent years, some countries have begun to measure the contribution of the creative and entertainment industries to GDP. In Kenya, USD$10 million in growth is projected in mobile music industry revenue between 2015 and 2020, and the South African music economy is expected to see annual growth of 4.4 per cent between 2015 and 2020 (Hruby, 2018). Overall, the African music industry is projected to double present-day revenue by 2020 to generate approximately USD$86 million a year.

The creative economy straddles economic, political, social, cultural and technological issues and is at the crossroads of the arts, business and technology. Moreover, the creative sector offers economic opportunities for women outside of education, which remains difficult for many to access. However, in order for this industry to achieve its full potential as a contributor to sustainable development, governments will need to increase measures to protect the arts and artists, including establishing better intellectual property protections and encouraging banks to fund creative projects. Nonetheless, the signs are promising, as two-thirds of African countries have signed the UNESCO Convention on the Protection and Promotion of the Diversity of Cultural Expressions (Hruby, 2018).

Conclusion

Although we can agree that Africa may be underachieving in many areas, there are also commendable achievements that are usually not publicised, and sectors of many African economies are engaged in rapid growth. The fact is that just like in every country, there are shanty towns and marks of poverty in African nations; however, that does not mean that everyone on the continent is poor. The effects of such perceptions have consequences for descendants of African heritage, whose self-esteem is impacted by these negative stereotypes, as well as for the reception and treatment of African migrants to Britain, who are perceived as parasites, rather than as major contributors to British society and culture. The publicity that abounds about negative occurrences makes it more difficult for Africans living abroad because the general impression is that if there is an incident in a certain region of a country, it is equally assumed that all parts of that country are affected, and that country is then labelled as a security risk. For example, although the Boko Haram insurgents mainly wreak havoc in the northern parts of Nigeria, many perceive the entire country as unsafe. Conflicts such as the wars in South Sudan, which deprived children of education and forced them into lives of poverty, should not be ignored; however, this does not mean that all children in Sudan are impacted by these wars. It is important to point out that some of these images do not represent the experiences of all children in Africa.

Africa is viewed as a poor 'country' (but Africa is a continent), with the implications being that when Africans visit European consular offices, they are sometimes treated with suspicion, and their motives for visiting developed countries are sometimes heavily scrutinised, notwithstanding their supporting documents. Africa is viewed as a corrupt 'country', so it is assumed that all Africans are corrupt. The view that all Africans are corrupt in turn results in African migrants being viewed with suspicion. Although it is acknowledged that some African countries are corrupt, and it is reported that more than USD $148 billion are lost annually to corruption in Africa, this is mostly due to the work of corrupt public officials, who are often funded by Europeans, Chinese, and multinational corporations, and not the actions of its citizens, many of who are searching for opportunities abroad due to the incessant corruption in their country of origin. The activities of a few criminals outside the African continent have also not helped the image of Black Africans. Despicable behaviours such as online dating fraud or agencies promising counterfeit visas to desperate immigrants make it difficult for some Black Africans living abroad, who must continue to prove their integrity by their conduct while at work or otherwise.

Many Africans in the diaspora had traumatic experiences in their countries of origin, such as those who came to Britain as war refugees. Some of these people have lost loved ones and hope to move on with their new lives in Britain. Returning to their country of origin is not an option, as they are in the UK to seek political asylum. However, reports of poor countries needing aid do not accurately portray what is happening in most African countries. Images of starved-looking children hawking for coins are regularly advertised on Western television to solicit for aid, and this outlook has not helped descendants of Africans in Britain to be proud of their heritage.

It is important to stress that there are other Black Britons who were born in the UK and have lived there throughout their lives. Such people have not developed links with any African country of origin, nor are they interested in doing so. Some of these people themselves also have children, and so their children follow their footsteps. Many young people self-define as 'Black British' rather than 'Black Ghanaian' or 'Black Nigerian' to avoid associations with the 'ghetto' stories that dominate their exposure to Africa. Some parents in the diaspora also contribute to such negative images when they threaten to send their children to African villages to frighten them into obedience, which reinforces unpleasant stereotypes for young Black Britons. In an ideal world, no one desires to be associated with the 'scum life' or the 'ghetto', and the more these images are shown in media without being balanced by the economic and social developments that are happening in Africa, the more it is difficult for young Britons to be interested in identifying with that continent.

Although stories of political and conflict refugees abound in Western news reports, in fact, the majority of Africans who migrate to developed countries, including the UK, do so in pursuit of viable jobs and education options. Africans take pride in education, and it is rather unfortunate that African universities continue to produce graduates who are unable to use the skills they have gained in the real world. Many African universities are still using older models of teaching to communicate with students, so that much of the knowledge that students gain during their undergraduate coursework cannot be used outside the classroom. The overall educational system in many African institutions is not fit for purpose. Many prospective recruiters have complained that African graduates are unable to produce curriculum vitae, exercise emotional intelligence and demonstrate archaic practises that do not fit into the standard behaviour of the new technologies operating in today's markets. Entrepreneur Fred Swaniker (2017), who heads the African Leadership Academy and the African Leadership University, has argued that in order to truly flourish, Africa needs educational systems that produce graduates who can immediately transfer academic knowledge to the real world and create jobs, rather than useless 'trophy certificate holders', who lack the skills to help the continent compete in the world economy.

For Africa to maintain steady economic, political, and social growth, governments must be willing to invest in their people. If African countries could create an enabling environment for people to be productive and thrive through the provision of relevant education and employment, more migrants might choose to remain home and help build regional economies. Improvement in the economies of African states would also encourage some members of the diaspora to return back to their country of origin to partake in nation building. However, as stated earlier in the chapter, citizens should also be proactive about their lives, and rather than merely blaming problems on bad governance. Globalisation has opened up opportunities for every individual to learn and develop new skills.

Secondly, Africa must be willing to address poverty and inequality. The enormous gap between the poor and the wealthy is a security risk, which is exacerbated by the corrupt and exploitative methods by which some have gained their wealth, thus discouraging hard work and fomenting resentment and anger.

Thirdly, the government must be willing to reduce its dependence on borrowing and foreign aid and start concentrating on its own resources—such as agriculture or the creative industries—as a means of generating revenues. Currently, foreign corporations and governments reap many of the benefits of Africa's vast natural and human resources, much as the US, Britain and Europe profited from the slave trade and colonialism. It is time for African governments to invest more fully in regional social and economic development in order to create more stable, productive societies in which communities can flourish and grow.

References

Adepoju, A. (1979). Migration and socio-economic change in Africa. *International Social Science Journal*, 31(2), 207-225.

Adegoke, Y. (2018). These will be Africa's fastest growing economies in 2018. World Economic Forum Retrieved from https://www.weforum.org/agenda/2018/01/what-does-2018-hold-for-african-economies

Amin, S. (1995). Migrations in contemporary Africa: A retrospective view. In J. Baker & T.A. Aina (eds.), *The migrant experience in Africa* (pp. 29-41). Uppsala: Nordiska Afhkainstitutet

Baker, J. & Aida, T.A. (Eds). (1995). *The migration experience in Africa*. Sweden: Nordiska Afrikainstitutet

Bekenova, K. (2016). Cultural and creative industries in Africa. *African Politics & Policy*, 2(2), http://orcid.org/0000-0002-9722-0311

Bratton, M., & van de Walle, N. (1997). *Democratic experiments in Africa: regime transitions in comparative perspective.* Cambridge: Cambridge University Press

Breeze, V., & Moore, N. (2017, 30 June). China has overtaken the US and UK as the top destination for Anglophone African students. *Quartz Africa*. Retrieved from https://qz.com/1017926/china-has-overtaken-the-us-and-uk-as-the-top-destination-for-anglophone-african-students

Busse, M., Erdogan, C., & Muhlen, H. (2014). China's impact on Africa, the Role of Trade, FDI and Aid. *Kyklos*, 69(2), 228–262.

Chutel, L. (2016, 23 November). Record unemployment affects these South Africans the most. *Quartz Africa*. Retrieved from https://qz.com/844825/south-africas-unemployment-rate-is-at-a-13-year-high-most-affecting-women-and-the-youth/

Donnelly, G. (2017, 29 November). What you don't know, but should, about the slave trade happening in Libya right now. *Fortune*. Retrieved from http://fortune.com/2017/11/29/libya-slave-trade/

Ehrhart, H., Le Goff, M., Rocher, E., & Singh, R. (2014). *Does migration foster exports? Evidence from Africa*. Policy Research Working Paper 6739. Washington, DC: The World Bank. Retrieved from https://openknowledge.worldbank.org/bitstream/handle/10986/16810/WPS6739.pdf;sequence=1

Elbagir, N., Razek, R., Platt, A., & Jones, B. (2017, 14 November). People for sale: Where lives are auctioned for $400. *CNN World*. Retrieved from https://www.cnn.com/2017/11/14/africa/libya-migrant-auctions/index.html

Fatunde, T. (2014, 30 May). Focus on Ghana shows 75,000 Nigerians studying there. *University World News*. Retrieved from http://www.universityworldnews.com/article.php?story=20140529173131311

Flahaux, M.-L. & De Haas, H. (2016). African migration: trends, patterns, drivers. *Comparative Migration Studies*, 4, 1. https://doi.org/10.1186/s40878-015-0015-6

Ghana Unemployment Rate 1991-2018. (2018). Trading economics. Retrieved from https://tradingeconomics.com/ghana/unemployment-rate

Hagen-Zanker,J.S. (2008). *Why do people migrate? A review of the theoretical literature*. MPRA Paper No. 28197. Maastricht Graduate School of Governance, Maastricht University Retrieved from https://mpra.ub.uni-muenchen.de/28197/1/2008WP002

Hagen-Zanker, J.S. (2010). *Modest expectations: Causes and effects of migration on migrant households in source countries* (Doctoral dissertation). Maastricht University. MGSoG Dissertation Series 5. Maastricht, NL: Boekenplan.

Honorati, M., & de Silva, S.J. (2016). Expanding job opportunities in Ghana. Direcռtions in Development. Washington, DC: World Bank. doi:10.1596/978-1-4648-0941-5.

Hruby, A. (2018 22 March). Tap creative industries to boost Africa's economic growth. *Financial Times*. Retrieved from https://www.ft.com/content/9807a468-2ddc-11e8-9b4b-bc4b9f08f381

Joseph-Aluko, O. (2016). Africans in the UK, Migration, Integration and Significance. London, UK: Author.

Kazeem, Y. (2016, 27 January). About half of the university graduates in Nigeria cannot find jobs. *Quartz Africa*. Retrieved from https://qz.com/603967/about-half-of-the-university-graduates-in-nigeria-cannot-find-jobs/

Kazeem, Y. (2017, 06 June). Nigeria's unemployment problem is showing no signs of slowing down. *Quartz Africa* (https://qz.com/999641/the-unemployment-rate-in-nigeria-has-climbed-for-nine-consecutive-quarters/).

Kambou, G. (2018). Global economic prospects – January 2018 – Economic outlook for the Sub-Saharan Africa region. Washington, D.C.: World Bank. Retrieved from http://pubdocs.worldbank.org/en/575011512062621151/Global-Economic-Prospects-Jan-2018-Sub-Saharan-Africa-analysis.pdf

Kuyok, K.A. (2017, 23 April). South Sudan's overseas students caught between a rock and a hard place. Times Higher Education. Retrieved from https://www.

timeshighereducation.com/blog/south-sudans-overseas-students-caught-between-rock-and-hard-place

Lensink, R. (1986). Structural adjustment in Sub -Saharan Africa (1st ed.). London: Longman.

Massey, D. S., Arango, J., Hugo, G., Kouaouci, A., Pellegrino, A., & Taylor, J.E. (1998). *Worlds in motion*. Oxford, Clarendon Press

McKinney, C.J. (2017, 6 March). Refugees in the UK. Retrieved from https://fullfact. org/immigration/uk-refugees/

Momodu, S. (December 2016-March 2017). Africa most affected by refugee crisis. *Africa Renewal Online*. Retrieved from http://www.un.org/africarenewal/magazine/december-2016-march-2017/africa-most-affected-refugee-crisis

Mora, J., & Taylor, J.E. (2005). Determinants of migration, destination, and sector choice: Disentangling individual, household and community effects. In Ç. Özden & M. Schiff (Eds.), *International migration, remittances and brain drain* (pp. 21-51). New York: Palgrave Macmillan.

Nigeria's unemployment rate rises from 14.2% to 18.8%. (2017, 23 December). *Vanguard*. Retrieved from https://www.vanguardngr.com/2017/12/nigerias-unemployment-rate-rises-14-2-18-8/

Offor, F. (2006). The quest for good governance in Africa: what form of democracy is most suitable? *The Journal of Social, Political, and Economic Studies*, 31(3), 265-277.

Shah, A. (2013, 23 March). Structural adjustment, a major cause of poverty. Retrieved from http://www.globalissues.org/article/3/structural-adjustment-a-major-cause-of-poverty

Shimeles, A. (2018). Understanding the patterns and causes of African migration: Some facts," by A. Shimeles. In B.S. Coulibaly (Ed.), Foresight Africa: Top priorities for the Continent in 2018 (pp. 54-57). Washington, D.C.: The Brookings Institution. Retrieved from https://www.brookings.edu/wp-content/uploads/2018/01/foresight-2018_full_web_final1.pdf

Shimeles, A. and T. Nabasaga. (2018). Why is inequality high in Africa. *Journal of African Economies*, forthcoming.

Sudan - Economic Indicators. (2018). Trading Economics. Retrieved from https:// tradingeconomics.com/sudan/indicators

Swaniker, F. (2017, 21 September). African universities: education with a purpose.

New African. Retrieved from http://newafricanmagazine.com/african-universi-ties-education-purpose/

Taiwo, S. (2017, 6 June). More Nigerian graduates become jobless, unemployment rate hits 21%. *The Pulse*. Retrieved from http://www.pulse.ng/bi/politics/unemployed-nigerians-more-nigerian-graduates-become-jobless-unemploy-ment-rate-hits-21-id6790778.html

Tanzania - Economic Indicators. (2018). Trading Economics. Retrieved from https://tradingeconomics.com/tanzania/indicators

Tharoor, I. (2017, 29 November). A 'slave auction' puts the global spotlight back on Libya. *Washington Post*. Retrieved from https://www.washingtonpost.com/news/worldviews/wp/2017/11/29/a-slave-auction-puts-the-global-spotlight-back-on-libya/?utm_term=.a0745bf37a1f

Unemployment in Africa: no jobs for 50% of graduates. (2016, 1 April). African Cen-tre for Economic Transformation. Retrieved from http://acetforafrica.org/high-lights/unemployment-in-africa-no-jobs-for-50-of-graduates/

UN Department of Economic and Social Affairs (UNDESA), Population Division (2013). *International Migration Report 2013*. Retrieved from http://www.un.org/en/development/desa/population/publications/pdf/migration/migra-tionreport2013/Full_Document_final.pdf

UN Department of Economic and Social Affairs (UNDESA), Population Division (2016). International Migration Report 2015: Highlights (ST/ESA/SER.A/375). Retrieved from http://www.un.org/en/development/desa/population/migra-tion/publications/migrationreport/docs/MigrationReport2015_Highlights.pdf

UN Department of Economic and Social Affairs (2018). Policy Brief #18: Achieving SDG 7 In Africa. Retrieved from https://sustainabledevelopment.un.org/con-tent/documents/17565PB18.pdf

UN Development Programme (UNDP) (2016). Human development indicators: Ken-ya. Retrieved from http://hdr.undp.org/en/countries/profiles/KEN

UN Educational, Scientific and Cultural Organization (UNESCO). (2017). Facts and figures: Sub-Saharan Africa's education progress and challenges. Retrieved from http://www.unesco.org/new/en/education/themes/leading-the-interna-tional-agenda/education-for-all/single-view/news/facts_and_figures_sub_sa-haran_africas_education_progress/

UN High Commission for Refugees (UNHCR). (1992). Persons covered by the OAU Convention Governing the Specific Aspects of Refugee Problems in Africa and by the Cartagena Declaration on Refugees. Retrieved from http://www.unhcr.org/en-us/excom/scip/3ae68cd214/persons-covered-oau-convention-governing-specific-aspects-refugee-problems.html

UN High Commission for Refugees (UNHCR). (2011-2018). Africa. Retrieved from http://www.unhcr.org/en-us/africa.html

UN High Commission for Refugees (UNHCR). (2011). The 1951 Refugee Convention and 1967 Protocol. Geneva: UNHCR. Retrieved from http://www.unhcr.org/en-us/about-us/background/4ec262df9/1951-convention-relating-status-refugees-its-1967-protocol.html

Verwimp, P. & Maystadt, J.F. (2015). Forced displacement and refugees in Sub-Saharan Africa: An economic inquiry. Policy Research Working Paper 7517. Washington, DC: The World Bank Group. (https://openknowledge.worldbank.org/bitstream/handle/10986/23481/Forced0displac00an0economic0inquiry.pdf?sequence=1

Weinstein, J. & Pillai, V.K. (2001). *Demography: the science of population*. Boston, MA: Allyn and Bacon.

'Where Are The Jobs? - Unemployment reaches unacceptable levels'. (2016, May 11). *The Finder*. Retrieved from http://www.peacefmonline.com/pages/business/news/201605/278792.php?storyid=100&

World Bank. (2013). Tourism in Africa: harnessing tourism for growth and improved livelihoods. Retrieved from https://www.worldbank.org/content/dam/Worldbank/document/Africa/Report/africa-tourism-report-2013-overview.pdf

Chapter 5.

<center>~~~</center>

The Mechanisms of Immigration Policy

This chapter begins with an overview of concepts of British nationality. It then provides a historical background of modern British immigration policies, including discussions of pre-9/11 policies and a review of how policies have evolved since those terrorist attacks, as the UK has sought to balance regard for human security with heightening concerns for its national security. Following this review, the chapter will provide an outline of the processes through which visas and naturalisation rights are obtained in Britain and describe some major forms of immigration abuses as well as other measures through which the government has attempted to limit the numbers of migrants entering or remaining in the country illegally.

Immigration has played a critical role in demographic changes throughout the UK, producing different waves of ethnic minorities and altering long-established patterns of social cohesion. Ethnic minorities face different barriers in the UK according to their migration trends, place of birth, generation and social status. The new immigration policies have resulted in setbacks for certain communities. For example, migrants from the EU countries are concerned about their status after Brexit, whereas those from the non-EU have been experiencing changes to policies that have denied many the rights to remain in the UK, and others the rights to settle down with their non-British spouses. Others experience problems like social morbidity and limited access to careers, education, housing and health. Many Caribbean migrants who have been settled in Britain for decades are finding it difficult to prove their status as legal residents;

as definitions of nationality have become more stringent, so have their associated paperwork and policies, and the scope of those 'belong' to Britain by right of birth is defined with increasing narrowness.

However, immigration policies are not a new phenomenon, and concerns about their enforcement have been ongoing. Protests against immigration are often based in measurements of migrant population growth published by statutory authorities, such as the notation that as of 2014, 13% of the UK population had been born abroad (Barr, 2016). More generally, the public outcry about migrants placing pressure on jobs has repeatedly motivated the government to reform immigration policies in order to put 'British workers' first. In the UK, controversy continues to follow many aspects of globalisation, ranging from questions about economic growth to a clamouring for more stringent policies, as seen in the ongoing debate about Brexit and its effects on trade and capital, as well as its potential impact on free movement by EU nationals. Immigration has also become an increasing concern as British people feel constrained both by workers from the EU and migrants from outside of Europe. Public opinions about immigration ultimately frame and shape policy responses in nation states, and the UK is not an exception to this trend.

Figure 4 shows a summary of the interaction between migration and migration policies. Immigration policies include any laws, rules, measures, and practises implemented by states concerning the transit of people across its borders, but especially those that intend to work and stay in the country. Immigration policies can range from allowing no migration at all to allowing most types of migration, such as free immigration. International migration policies thus have the objective of influencing the volume, origin and internal composition of immigration flows (Czaika & De Haas). This may include increasing or decreasing numbers or maintaining current levels, as well as efforts to change the composition of migrants' countries (or regions) of origin. Such policies may also include a level of 'skills bias', whereby migrants are admitted based on the skills that they can bring to the UK. Recent immigration policies in the UK have been in favour of highly skilled migrants, because it is assumed that these groups of migrants would represent benefits for the UK economy.

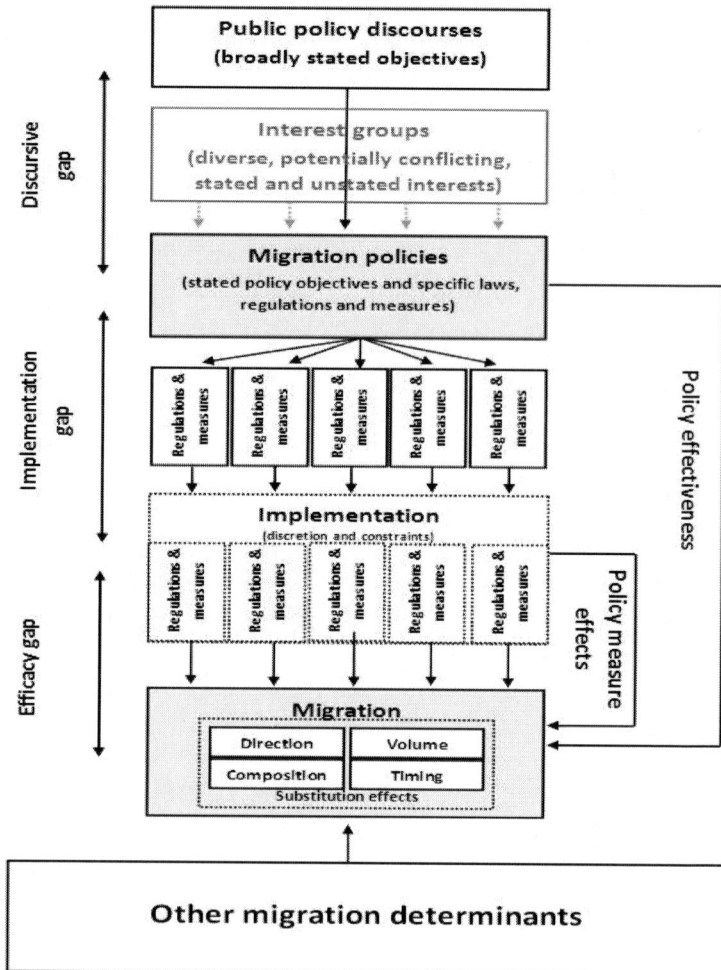

Figure 4.[6] Migration policy effects and effectiveness

---

[6] Reprinted from Strangers & citizens: a positive approach to migrants and refugees, by Sarah Spencer. London, UK: IPPR/Rivers Oram Press.

Conceptualisations of British Nationality

Nationality is defined as the status of belonging to a particular country by birth or naturalisation. Nationality encompasses the relationship between a person and their state of origin, culture, association, affiliation and or loyalty. Nationality affords the state jurisdiction over a person and in turn endows the person with the state's protection. For instance, if a British citizen encounters troubles in another country, the British government can advocate for that citizen and see that they are allowed to return to the UK.

In medieval times, pride in citizenship was historically associated with belief in equality, freedom and self-government; however, in modern times, the concept has been distorted in many of our nation-states into a very different sort of belief that a citizen is naturally and properly superior to an alien, and that inequality between citizens and aliens is a part of the natural order (Juss, 1994). Historically, although such views have tended to remain dormant during times of economic prosperity or relative security, anti-immigrant hostility has always become more active during periods of recession or conflict, when the citizen feels their economic or physical security to be threatened by the 'aliens' in their midst.

Overview of British Nationality

There is no distinct definition of British nationality. Professor Clive Parry declared that 'there is not and never has been any domestic concept of British nationality as such' (Parry, 1957, p. 5). Indeed, notions of Englishness and Britishness have shifted historically depending upon the territorial expanse of the state and its dominant religion, and the dynamic relationship between national identity, nationality, and citizenship in Britain has manifested in various ways.

Medieval Britain had a long-standing reliance on the rule of the birth-place, whereby citizenship was in theory determined based on *juis soli* and the rule of descent, *juis sanguinis* (Dummett & Nicol, 1990). In fact, however, conferment of citizenship was based on personal allegiance to the crown. Allegiance to the crown made a person a crown subject, and the status of subject was given to those born within the crown's territories (Dummett & Nicol, 1990). Over time, special arrangements were made foreigners and the children of subjects who were born abroad to become subjects.

Today, British nationality has great practical importance as defined by law (Dummet and Nicol 1990). As a concept, British nationality is quite ephemeral; however, as a lived-experience, its expressions can be highly perceptible. In the UK, an individual's nationality comes into play in two main instances. At the most elementary, physical level, nationality is examined through immigration clearance forms at airports, which determine who lines up where and who is allowed instant right of passage. Second, in recent years, the question of nationality has come to be more emphasised in accessing basic services such as the NHS or bank account opening services, or even obtaining an education or renting a place to live. Thus, a person's legal status defines their legitimacy to nationality. Unlike countries such as the USA, the status of citizenship is not defined by nationhood in the UK, and Britain permits a person to have a dual national relationship. For example, a child born in Antigua whose parent is a British citizen automatically acquires British citizenship by birth alongside their Antiguan citizenship (Karatani, 2003).

As exemplified by the British Nationality Act 1981, being a citizen of UK conveys British nationality on that individual, which confers the inherent right of abode in Britain. A British national is aware of his or her right to no restriction of movement in and out of the United Kingdom, along with other civil, political and social rights, including the conventional British passport. People who do not have the British citizenship or a settlement visa may have restrictions placed on them. These restrictions are technically referred to as 'immigration control'.

Contrary to popular belief, the potential of immigration to expose the nerve of national identity and raise questions about nationality is deeply rooted in British history. There has been much public debate concerning nationality and immigration, which has largely been triggered by the influx of migrants from both European and non-European nation states. What is the correlation between immigration and nationality? Nations have always attributed problems that arise in their nation to overpopulation, especially when there is mass unemployment, inflation, religious riots and so on. This in turn leads the nation to make determinations on whether to close its borders or to review who is entitled to its nationality. Hence, we cannot talk about nationality without referring to immigration.

Nationalisation and Early British Immigration Policies

For much of its history, Britain actually operated an unplanned open-door immigration policy, and no restrictions were placed on the freedom of movement of aliens unless they were criminals. The Naturalisation Act 1844 marked the beginning of the modern process of naturalisation by establishing the procedure through which foreigners could obtain national status as granted by the Secretary of State. During the remainder of the 19th century and the first half of the 20th century, further legislation was enacted concerning both the recognition and grant of British subject status. From 1847 onwards, a person naturalised in the UK obtained imperial naturalisation, which conferred British subject status throughout the British Empire (Seddon, 2006, p. 1402). This measure was among the earlier attempts to formulate a strategy or process by which those designated as British could be given a sense of a common identity.

In the latter half of the 19th century, the crackdown against anarchists and other accused agitators in many European countries displaced many people, and it seemed only natural then for Britain to absorb such refugees into its midst (Dummet & Nicol, 1990). However, this open-door policy ended with the introduction of the Aliens Act 1905, which was passed to curb Jewish immigration from the pogroms of tsarist Russia and to prevent the massive rise in unemployment caused by the refugee influx (Juss, 1994). However, immigration remained open to those within the Empire, as exemplified by the British Nationality and Status of Aliens Act 1914, which granted the common status of British subject upon any individual connected with the Crown's dominions. This foundered as the British Empire fell apart, and with the development of the Commonwealth of Nations in 1921, the single imperial status of British subject became increasingly inadequate to deal with the realities of a Commonwealth with independent member states. Over the years, as colonised peoples increased their resistance to imperial control, Britain found it more difficult to maintain political cohesion as territories that had been settled by British people began to break away and become independent and establish their own citizenship laws. For example, in 1946, Canada created its own Canadian citizenship, which was separate from the status of British subject. In 1948, the Commonwealth Heads of Government agreed that each member would adopt a national citizenship; however, the existing status of British subject would continue to be a common status held by all Commonwealth citizens. This was codified as the British Nationality Act 1948, which granted colonials rights as 'Citizens of the United Kingdom and Colonies' (CUKCs).

The Windrush Generation: Nationalisation in the Twilight of Empire

There have always been pockets of Black people in Britain; however, it was only in the latter part of the twentieth century that the Black population began to grow sufficiently to feature prominently in the country's demographic composition. Following the end of the Second World War in 1945, Britain required labour to re-build the economy, and its leaders were obliged to acknowledge that an influx of immigrants was needed to accomplish this goal. Accordingly, people from the Caribbean were invited to take up these vacancies. The Caribbeans migrants paved the way for the increase of the UK's Black population, beginning when the 'Empire Windrush' first docked in 1948. Subsequently, there were other migrations flows from India and Pakistan and West Africa. These groups of immigrants constituted only one percent of the UK's population, and they were not well accepted within the White communities. These Caribbean migrants were placed in conditions where they worked long hours, and they were frequently denied housing and other services based on their colour. Moreover, they were subject to harassment and violent attacks from local youths.

By the mid-1960s, approximately 75,000 immigrants a year were arriving in Britain, much to the displeasure and chagrin of the White natives, who were not prepared to see foreign races in their midst and started lobbying politicians to restrict immigration from 'coloured people'. The government responded to these demands with the 1962 Commonwealth Immigrants Act, which removed the automatic rights of immigration for all Commonwealth citizens without a connection to the UK (including Citizens of the United Kingdom and Colonies who were not born in the UK and not holding a British passport issued by the British government); thus, making them subject to immigration control. A number of negative assumptions were made against the Black population, which further fuelled racial tensions. This was the case in the West Midlands, for example, where many of the White community expressed resistance at the idea of living amidst Black people. Capitalising off of this xenophobia, during the 1964 election, Conservative MP Peter Griffiths employed the campaign slogan 'if you want a nigger for a neighbour, vote Liberal or Labour' and narrowly won after what was described as one of the most racist political campaigns in British history (Woods, 2016). It is not until the late 1960s and particularly the 1970s -1980s that the Black population began to make a demographic imprint in most major cities in the UK, and their presence continued to be met with opposition, as British natives claimed that these immigrants were driving down jobs and housing.

Role of the Windrush Generation in Founding the National Health Service

Black people have played a central role in the National Health Service (NHS) since its founding. The NHS was established as part of the reconstruction effort following the Second World War. Previously, healthcare was available only to those with the means to afford it, thus resulting in severe inequities and enormous suffering among poor Britons from the effects of poor nutrition and disease. After the war, Aneurin Bevan, the Labour Minister of Health, conceived of a system whereby the entire nation would contribute to free health care through a National Insurance plan, and the NHS was officially established in 1948. However, as noted above, the war had left Britain with severe labour shortages, and the government found it impossible to staff the 2688 hospitals that it had taken over with the passing of the National Health Service Act (Dent, 2018). Amidst the post-War economic boom, it was extremely difficult to recruit men to work for the NHS, which primarily offered lower paying jobs for long hours in poor conditions, and the newly independent single women could also afford to be more selective about their career choices, and most took up occupations in white collar positions such as secretaries and journalists.

Thus, it was necessary to recruit the staff for the Service from the colonies, particularly those in the Caribbean, and in 1949, the Ministries of Health and Labour, the Colonial Office, the General Nursing Council (GNC) and the Royal College of Nursing began collaborating to attract women and men from the Caribbean and other colonies to apply for work as hospital auxiliaries, nurses and trainee nurses, and domestic workers. Thousands of recruits responded during the 1950s and 1960s, many paying their own fares, and were trained to the highest levels in their profession according to British standards. Most found themselves assigned not to the General or teaching hospitals staffed by White Britons, but rather trained in institutions dedicated to the care of the chronically sick, disabled and the elderly, as well as psychiatric hospitals, where populations had increased dramatically due to the massive impact of post-war trauma.

Despite the country's enormous need for these clinicians, many of whom already had the requisite qualifications, racial discrimination was a strong factor in the training they received, and most Caribbeans and Black British nurses were placed on the two-year 'Pupil' or

State-Enrolled Nursing (SEN) course, which focused on lower-paid clinical nursing and offered fewer opportunities for promotion, rather than the more advanced 'Staff' or State Registered Nurse (SRN) qualification programme, which included training in ward management and other leadership duties (Ramdin, 1987). The trainees lived in Nurses' Homes attached to the hospitals, and most settled in large cities with already existing African and Caribbean populations. By 1966, there were an estimated 3,000-5,000 Jamaican nurses working in British hospitals (Snow & Jones, 2011). Although many had planned to return home after receiving their training, their options were limited by the SEN course, which was not recognised outside Britain, and efforts to obtain the full training were usually rebuffed.

The NHS has perennially experienced additional staffing crises since its founding, and it has continued to recruit clinical staff from its former colonies even amidst tightening immigration controls. As recently as 2018, the British Government has engaged with Jamaica to send nurses as part of an international programme aimed at recruiting 5500 nurses (Ford, 2018). From the 1960s, physicians and ancillary staff have also recruited from across Britain's colonies and former colonies, particularly from South Asia, and these were similarly marginalised into lower-paying positions in provincial hospitals (Ramdin, 1987). Currently, nearly a third of the clinicians in the NHS are from Black and minority ethnic groups, among whom 30% of junior doctors and 40% of nurses were born outside the UK (Snow & Jones, 2011). Regardless of their qualifications and experience, however, BME doctors and nurses are primarily concentrated in the lower professional grades and work in less popular areas and occupy fewer than 10% of NHS senior manager jobs and only 1% of NHS chief executive positions (Snow & Jones, 2011).

The Intensification of Controls: British Immigration Policies, 1960-2001

Before the late 1960s, despite the discrimination and related indignities they faced, migration to the UK remained relatively simple for those born in its colonies, including Africans, as there was little if any difference in the law between the rights of CUKCs and other British subjects, all of whom had the right to enter and live in the United Kingdom at any time. As noted in Chapters 3 and 4, a number of African and Caribbean students were thus able to obtain university educations in the UK. However, immigration laws have become increasingly stringent over the past several decades, and more and more regulations have been established to limit British nationality.

As colonialism began ending in the British colonies, many Black students returned to help rebuild their countries of origin; however, another migration for education began in the late 1960s-early 1970s, which in Nigeria was fuelled by the prosperity of the oil boom, which increased the number of students who could pay British university fees. Some of these students attempted to return to their home countries in the 1970s to obtain employment there; however, their return home could not be sustained, as the economic situation in most of the West African countries began to deteriorate and jobs were scarce even for educated people. Many industries and infrastructures collapsed through incompetent political leadership and corruption, which resulted in a massive brain drain to Britain and other Western nations.

As many people from countries like Nigeria, Sierra-Leone, and Ghana began to migrate to Britain, White Britons began to feel threatened by the mass immigration of people from Africa in search of jobs. Britain began closing its borders to people of colour, and over the decades, the British government has introduced various immigration controls to reduce the number of foreign people that migrated to Britain. Throughout the history of Black migration to Britain, different legislations have been introduced to manage the vast and complex flows of 'alien' people into the UK. The first step to closing the door on Black immigrants and establishing racial inequality in the operation of the law was enacted through the 1962 Commonwealth Immigrants Act, which distinguished between British citizens in the Empire and those born on UK soil and imposed immigration controls on all Commonwealth citizens without a connection to the UK, including Citizens of the United Kingdom and Colonies who were not born in the UK and lacked a British passport issued by the British government. Commonwealth citizens who were residing in the UK or who had resided in the UK at any point from 1960 to 1962 were exempted, as well as CUKCs and Commonwealth citizens holding a passport issued by the British government or who were born in the UK. This was amended by the Commonwealth Immigrants Act 1968, which further reduced rights of citizens of countries in the Commonwealth of Nations by prohibiting their ability to enter Britain without work vouchers, which were of course limited in number.

However, it was the 1971 Immigration Act that demonstrated the specific operation of a colour bar in British law. The 1971 Act rested on the concept of patriality, which meant that only those with direct personal or ancestral connections with Britain had the right to live there. Coloured immigration was virtually halted, whereas the right of entry remained intact for White citizens of the old Commonwealth, such as those from Australia, New Zealand and Canada. Similar rights of entry were provided to persons with freedom of movement in the

European Community in the Immigration Act 1988. However, the British Nationality Act 1981, which came into effect on 1 January 1983, changed previous rules granting such to any citizen of the UK and Colonies by birth, descent, legal adoption, naturalisation or registration in the UK and established the current system of multiple categories of British nationality, which comprises British citizens, British overseas territories citizens, British overseas citizens, British nationals (overseas), British subjects, and British protected persons. A person holding a British passport might have any of the above national statuses.

Over the decade and a half between 1979 and 1995, the number of people seeking entry to Britain based on political asylum increased dramatically, perhaps partly in response to the above restrictions, but also due to the spread of violent conflicts and other crises in many African countries. While in 1979, only 1563 people applied to Britain for political asylum, by 1995, that figure had reached nearly 45,000 (Blinder, 2017). The percentage of individuals granted full refugee status declined in response; however, some applicants received 'exceptional leave' based on such compassionate grounds such as family ties, and many remained undiscouraged because the lengthy delays in processing their applications made them more eligible for concessions. The UK Government's policy on immigration and nationality was set out in the Immigration and Nationality Department Annual Report (1995) published just before the Asylum and Immigration Act of 1996, which made it a criminal offence to employ anyone lacking the legal right to live and work in the country and also limited welfare benefits to those asylum seekers had who applied on arrival at a UK port (though the latter rule was overturned on appeal (Home Department, 1998). This policy stated several priorities, including: 1) to allow genuine visitors and students to enter the United Kingdom; 2) to give effect to the free movement provisions of European Community law; 3) to continue to admit the spouses and dependent children of those already settled in the United Kingdom; yet also to 4) to severely restrict the numbers coming to live permanently or to work in the United Kingdom; and 5) to maintain an effective and efficient system for dealing with applicants for citizenship (Spencer, 1998, p. 85). With respect to people seeking asylum, the report stated its intentions

to meet the United Kingdom's obligations towards refugees under international law, while reducing the scope and incentive for misusing asylum procedures. When an individual does not qualify for refugee status, their individual circumstances will be considered and leave to remain granted in exceptional cases (Home Office, 1995).

Three years later, actions against asylum seekers intensified with the passing of the Immigration and Asylum Act 1999, which aimed to make the process of seeking asylum 'fairer, faster and firmer' through streamlining and strengthening pre-entry controls and the prosecution of those providing immigration officials with 'a tissue of lies' (Home Office, 1999) based on seeking asylum for economic reasons, as well as reducing the rights of appeal available to those whose applications are rejected. The Act of 1999 minimised cash payments to £10 weekly for adult asylum seekers and replaced the welfare benefits with vouchers worth £35 a week, as well as restricting immigration for marriage purposes ('Immigration and Asylum Act 1999,' 2009). Moreover, under the administration of the newly created National Asylum Service, eligibility for support required asylum seekers to agree to be dispersed away from areas with large communities, including many migrants, such as London or Dover, to areas with a surplus of unused housing stock, which were of course those cities suffering from economic decline and high levels of crime and violence, much of which was directed towards the asylum seekers themselves, who were perceived as an invasive strain on already reduced local resources ('Immigration and Asylum Act 1999,' 2009).

The Post-9/11 Immigration Climate

After the September 11 terrorist attacks in the USA, calls for stronger immigration controls resounded in many Western countries, including the UK. In Britain, these controls began with the Nationality, Immigration and Asylum Act 2002, which cracked down on 'sham' marriages and introduced the country's first English test and citizenship exam for any immigrant who wished to apply for naturalisation or Indefinite Leave to Remain in the UK. Since 28 July 2004, applicants for naturalisation on grounds of marriage or five years residence are required to have sufficient knowledge of English, Welsh or Scottish Gaelic. The test creates a significant barrier for a significant number of migrants born in non-English speaking countries, who might not be able to speak or read English fully as a language. Certainly, this is the case for many older candidates who may be illiterate in their own mother tongues, let alone in English. In November 2004, the Government set up a new board, the Advisory Board on Naturalisation and Integration (ABNI) to provide independent advice to the Government on its citizenship and integration programme. In November 2005, the ABNI oversaw the introduction of the 'Life in the UK Test', which tests migrants' knowledge on British values, history, traditions and everyday life. Test takers must receive scores of at least 75% to pass. One exception to this rule is that migrants from EU countries need only take the test if applying for citizenship, and they are exempt if merely requesting Indefinite Leave to Remain.

The citizenship exam has been heavily criticised based on containing factual errors, as well as charges that it includes a number of questions that even British citizens are unable to answer. A clear point of debate concerning the test is the extent to which indigenous British citizens would either be able to pass the test or would want to take the pledge of loyalty. In a 2012 exercise, for example, every single member of the editorial team of the *New Statesman* news organisation failed the exam (Hasan, 2012). Another issue has been the large numbers of fraud cases occurring in association with the exam, whereby people have been prosecuted for selling pass certificates to migrants (Kemp, 2008, 04 April; 'Men Jailed for UK Citizenship Fraud in Sheffield', 2010) or taking the tests on others' behalf (Kemp, 2008, 05 April; 'Test Faker Conman Is Jailed,' 2011). Interestingly, statistics on pass rates have noted significant variations based on the original nationalities and cultures of the candidates, whereby for 2013-2014, the highest levels, above 95%, were achieved only by exam takers from other Western countries, including Australia, Canada, New Zealand, and the United States, and pass rates for EU citizens during this period averaged 86% (Home Office, 2014). Much lower rates have been recorded for candidates from African nations, with the highest occurring among former British colonies such as Kenya (75%), Botswana (71%) Nigeria (69%), Ghana (65%) and Benin (64%), though candidates from the Gambia (54%), Sierra Leone (54%) and Liberia (57%) have tended to pass at lower rates (Home Office, 2014). These differences may be partly attributed to the closer cultural ties between the Western countries and the UK, as well as the greater levels of social marginalisation from mainstream British life occurring among migrants from non-Western countries.

The Immigration, Asylum and Nationality Act 2006 introduced a number of limitations to the appeals process, such as restricting the right of appeal for refusal of entry clearance in cases where the subject intends to enter the country as a dependent, a visitor or a student, so that appeals are only available for those seeking asylum based on human rights and race discrimination grounds. The 2006 Act also made further changes to nationality law, widening the power to deprive a person of citizenship or the right of abode if considered 'conducive to the public good', which had previously only applied to non-Britons, to encompass dual citizens, including those actually born in the UK (Cobain, 2011). The Act removed registration as a British citizen as of right by inserting a good character test for all applicants, and an Order passed in January 2010 included children aged ten and over in the 'good character requirement'. Children were also targets of the UK Borders 2007, which brought in the power to create compulsory biometric cards for non-EU immigrants, including those aged under 16, and granted immigration officers police-like powers, such as increased detention and a search-and-entry roles, while the UK Border Agency was enabled to automatically deport some foreign nationals imprisoned for specific offences, or for more than one year 'UK Borders Act 2007,', 2009). Two years later, the Borders, Citizenship and Immigration Act 2009 targeted sham marriages by making it so that people applying for naturalisation after marriage were required to wait five years after residency, while all others from outside the Eurozone were obliged to have residential status for eight years. Additionally, whereas previously, those living in the UK for at least five years were eligible to apply for Indefinite Leave to Remain, these migrants were now limited to 'probationary citizenship', with full naturalisation pending the earning of 'points' through such good works as community volunteering or civic participation through trade union activities or canvassing for a political party, as well as moving to areas less populated with immigrants or temporarily returning home to share skills ('Citizenship points plan launched,' 2009).

Recent Changes in Immigration Policies

Since 1997, immigration has been a primary issue—often number one or number two—mentioned in British opinion polls, and in 2012, the British Social Attitudes Survey found that 52% of respondents viewed migrants as having a negative economic impact of migrants, while a full 75% supported a reduction in immigration (Figure 5.2). The new immigration policies introduced by the Home Office that year were declared as a marker of Conservative response to these sentiments. On 9 July 2012, a number of changes to the UK Immigration Rules came into effect. The new reforms fully incorporated the Points Based System (PBS), which changed the criteria and routes by which non-EU migrants are admitted into the UK. These measures have impacted migration from all non-EU countries on a global scale, including people from some European countries, Commonwealth countries such as Australia and Jamaica, America, Asia, including the Middle East, and of course the continent of Africa. The categories of people who are impacted include international students, workers and the dependant relatives of those who already have a 'settled status' in the UK, such as British nationals and those with indefinite leave to remain. By creating and updating the sets of requirements to be filled before an individual can achieve status to obtain an indefinite leave to remain or naturalisation to become a British citizen, the new measures have made it difficult for even legal immigrants to remain in the UK through their complex financial requirements and thresholds, which very few immigrants are able to fulfil. For example, whereas previously, only applicants for citizenship had to meet knowledge requirements, on October 2013, the UK Border Agency (UKBA) introduced additional rules requiring all non-exempt applicants for settlement in the UK to pass the Life in the UK Test and an intermediate level English language test at the B1 level or above. ('British Citizenship Test tightened to Include English Test,' 2013).

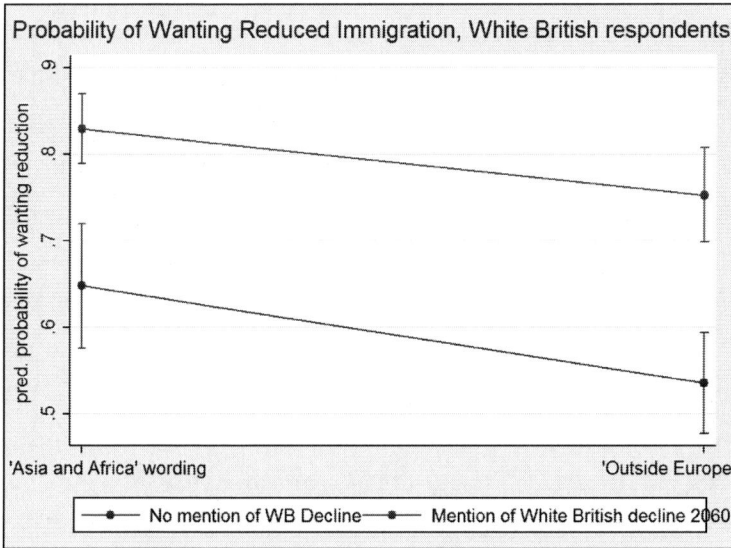

Figure 5. Attitudes towards reduced immigration (Kaufman, 2018)

The UK uses a range of mechanisms to exercise immigration control, including immigration policies, border controls, administrative removals, detention, deportation, and hostile environment. For the purposes of this chapter, I will highlight the 'hostile environment' component, which is a term coined by then-Home Secretary Theresa May for an official policy introduced in 2012 aimed at making it difficult for illegal immigrants to remain in the UK (Travis, 2013). The purpose of the hostile environment policy was to discourage illegal immigration and to encourage them to voluntarily return back to their country of origin. Some of these measures are encoded in the Immigration Acts 2014 and 2016, such as new limits on access to work, whether paid or unpaid, the introduction of NHS surcharges, prohibitions on housing, and more recently freezing of the bank accounts of illegal immigrants. However, although these policies are ostensibly aimed at illegal immigrants, other ethnic minorities residing legally in the UK are sometimes also soft targets, particularly in the area of housing. It is not uncommon for certain landlords to discriminate against Black and minority ethnic people when they are seeking to rent or buy a house. Of course, except by proof of identity, which an ordinary citizen has no right to ask of anyone in the public, there is no way one can know if the Black or the Asian person living next to you is a Black British or Asian British. This hinders good community relations and can lead to unnecessary suspicion of Black and minority ethnic groups. According to research conducted in the West Midlands in 2015, some landlords displayed potentially discriminatory behaviour or attitudes, and Black, Asian and Minority Ethnic tenants were more likely than Whites to be asked for their immigration papers. Apart from this, the need to show proof of identity in opening bank accounts or in registering for GP services and other public services has restricted British citizens who lack passports or other documentation because it was not relevant at the time, such as many members of the 'Windrush generation' who came to the UK during the 1940s, leaving them without access to healthcare, housing, or benefits and vulnerable to the constant threat of being detained and deported.

In addition to the above measures are the astronomical, continually increasing fees for those applying for leave to remain, indefinite leave to remain and other routes to remain in the UK. The newer rules have made applying for leave to remain more expensive for migrants, thus further constricting routes further for many non-EU migrants. Since 2015, the government has instituted an NHS surcharge on all new applications for leave to remain in the UK, which is payable at the time of application. Initially, students were required to pay £150, while all others were charged £200, meaning that a family of six people with four children would have to pay £1,200 in NHS surcharges. In early 2018, the UK government announced plans to double that surcharge to £400 per person (Syal, 2018).

Restricting the Family Route

The immigration policies have impacted upon genuine marriages and families, as a consequence of which some families have been forced to live apart with dire consequences for the individuals and their children. The term 'families' in this context refers to dependants of international students, children of British citizens/legal immigrants/ refugees, and adult dependant relatives like aged parents. Prior to the introduction of these policies, there were no stringent financial threshold attached to family routes. An income threshold of £18,600 per year before tax has now been introduced for sponsoring the settlement in the UK of a non-EEA spouse, fiancé or proposed civil partner, with the threshold increasing by £2,400 for each sponsoring child in the relationship. The Joint Council for the Welfare of Immi- grants (2016) indicated that 41% of British population citizens would not qualify under the new income requirement. In addition, the gov- ernment has published a list of factors associated with genuine and non-genuine relationships to help UK Border Agency officers make accurate decisions and extended the minimum probationary period for settlement for non-EEA spouses and partners from two years to five years in order to test the 'genuineness' of their relationships. In cases when a couple has been living together overseas for at least four years, the new rules abolished the permission for immediate set- tlement for migrant spouses and partners. The aim of such measures is to cut down the number of immigrants from outside the European Union, but it appears that many British nationals are being penalised for forming relationships with those from countries outside the EU, resulting in both moral and emotional devastation for those families unable to live together due to the new rules, as spouses become forcibly divided and children are forced to be separated from one of their parents. The government itself estimated that the new rules will break up as many as 17,800 families every year (Home Office, 2012). The UK government claims to be supportive of families and in favour of the institution of marriage; however, the best interests of the child within a family setting do not appear to have been taken into consideration with the institution of such measures, as children must now face growing up with the support of their parents, which could lead to enormous damage to the development and wellbeing.

The rules also impact other family relationships, so that adult and elderly dependants can only settle in the UK if they can demonstrate that they require a level of long-term personal care that can only be provided by a relative in the UK based on age, illness or disability, and they must apply from overseas. Family visit visa appeals have been restricted by narrowing the current definitions of family and sponsor for appeal purposes, and then, subject to the passage of the Crime and Courts Bill, removing the full right of appeal against refusal of a family visit visa. The English language test requirement also applies to immigrant spouses before they are allowed to join their partners in the UK. This disqualifies immigrants from some areas of Europe and other countries for whom English is not their first language from joining their families in the UK.

Case study 1

F and A are Sierra Leoneans with two children ages 10 and 14 years. F moved to the UK with the six-year-old. She came in as a student nurse. She returns to Uganda every six months to see her family. Her income is about £28,500, so she meets the income threshold. Following her confirmation of leave to remain in the UK, she proceeded to apply for her husband and her six-year-old child to join her in the UK. Her application was refused because they were not convinced that she was married to A or that the six-year-old child was hers. During this period F experienced a lot of anxiety and it impacted upon her ability to take care of her child who was attending school with unkempt hair. F also had started missing work. It took the help of a member of the community to step into F's situation when the school were demanding answers. F's daughter would have been placed under a child protection. Eventually, the local authority stepped into the situation and after much documentation across countries and solicitors' involvement, F's husband was eventually allowed to join his family.

Case study 2

Q is a Sudanese national, who came to the UK as a refugee, due to threats made to his life over his political views. He fled South Sudan leaving his wife and two children behind. After obtaining his asylum and eventual ILR (Indefinite leave to remain), he applied for his wife and children to join him. Q works as an Estate surveyor, earning between £30,000-£32,000. His wife attended the interview for the application, but her application was turned down because she could not speak English and needed an interpreter. The wife explained that there was no English school in her vicinity, and she had to travel far leaving her children, and this was not feasible considering the tension in Sudan.

Cutting off Workers and Students

Previous immigration rules made it easier for workers to obtain permits to obtain employment as well as allowing more students to enter the country and providing them with opportunities to enter into the labour market once they complete their studies or extend their studies. Now, however, students attending higher education institutions and language schools face new restrictions not included in the previous application process. It is now required that they possess a higher standard of English language skills before entry, and it is imperative that any educational institution that wants to sponsor international students have proper accreditation. As described above, the government has instituted a requirement for workers to obtain a work permit according to the point based system. The previous post-study work visa has now been converted to a form of Tier 2 visa, and most students are encouraged to return to their home countries once they finish their studies.

Case study 3

P was an American national and was an employee of a particular mobile phone company. P has worked with the organisation since he was a student. On graduating from university, based on good standing with the organisation, he was invited to head the marketing unit of the company. P had a permit to work for another 12 months following his graduation. Shortly before the expiration of his work permit, P applied to the home office for an extension of his visa, but his visa application was refused. P was told that his employer had to show proof that he could not get another British national who could do the same job. P regrettably had to resign his appointment, and he returned to the US. P said although he loved the UK, and the experience, he is not willing to waste his money in fighting the immigration system as he knows he cannot win in the UK.

The Immigration Process and Visa Routes

This section examines the process of how a person lacking any of the six different forms of British nationality (see above) can become a British citizen. Under the Immigration Act 1981, British nationality can be obtained in three ways, by birth, descent or adoption, registration and naturalisation (Seddon, 2006). Legislation enacted in 2009 (The British Citizenship and Immigration Act 2009) enabled registration as British of the children of members of the armed forces born outside the UK and confirms automatic British citizenship of children of armed forces members born in the UK. Registration of children born outside the UK was extended from 12 months (or six years in exceptional circumstances) up to their 18th birthday and registration was enabled for those born before 7 February 1961 with British mothers, as during that period women did not have the same legal rights as men to pass on their citizenship status to their children.

Under IA 2014, from 6 April 2015, registration as a British citizen was enabled for all those who were not registered as British citizens at birth because their parents were unmarried. However, generally, nationality rules have become increasingly more stringent over the past two or three decades such that now, as mentioned above, it is compulsory for anyone who seeks to naturalise as a British citizen to pass the life in the UK test.

The UK Work Permit

Historically, the UK had a tradition of issuing work permits to specific applicants seeking to fill in vacancies or gain working experience. Between the 1950s and the 1960s, people were issued with vouchers until the system was changed to become based on permits in 1971 (see above). The work permit system required a valid job offer from a viable employer in the UK and tended to favour highly skilled sectors, such as computer/IT related occupations, health associate professionals and other health/medical occupations, and managers and administrators; however, it was also extended to seasonal agricultural workers in 2002.

After spending a number of years in Britain, the work permit holder could apply for Indefinite Leave to Remain and for their spouses or other dependants to join them in the UK; these dependants were able to work in the country without restriction. Through such schemes, many foreign nationals were able to take up employment in different sectors in the UK, and hundreds of thousands of migrants entered Britain through this system over the decades; for instance, in 2002 a total of 129,041 work permits were issued, and this number was exceeded in 2003. The UK work permit was used as a route by other entrants into the UK until November 2008, when the five-tier system was introduced.

Points-Based-Immigration

Any non-citizen who wishes to come to the UK either temporarily or permanently must obtain a visa to be admitted. Since 2008, the UK has employed a five-tier visa system for applicants outside the Eurozone, which consists of the following work, study, and investment visas ('UK Five Tier Points-Based Immigration System,' 2018). This points-based system is the primary UK immigration route for migrants from outside the European Economic Area (EEA) to come to the UK to work, study, invest or train.

Tier 1 visa: This visa category applies to 'high-value migrants' who are eligible for the 'exceptional talent' visa, such graduates of UK universities who are endorsed by their university or by the UK government's Trade and Investment Department, as well as those endorsed by the Home Office as a leader or emerging leader in the fields of science, humanities, engineering, medicine, digital technology or the arts. This category also includes successful entrepreneurs and investors, for which regulations respectively require minimum investments of £50,000 and £2,000,000 for qualified applicants.

The Entrepreneur Route

To be eligible for an entrepreneur visa, applicants must demonstrate that they have sufficient funding for investment in a business, and are required to supply a business plan, which will be scrutinised for viability by civil servants at the Home Office. The initial visa is valid for about three years, which can be extended for another two years before an application for settlement can be made, though an 'accelerated settlement' can also be processed within three years if the business is particularly successful or creates a certain number of full-time jobs ('Tier 1 (Entrepreneur) visa,' n.d.). By the same token, the entrepreneur is required to create the equivalent of 2 full-time (30 hours per week) paid jobs for at least two people during the visa period, and each job must exist for at least 12 months ('Tier 1 (Entrepreneur) visa,' n.d.).

The amount required to be invested in the business depends on the source of the funds. Persons with access to £50,000 in investment funds from a registered venture capital firm, a UK entrepreneurial seed funding competition endorsed by the Department for International Trade (DIT) or a UK government department that has funds available to set up or expanding a UK business ('Tier 1 (Entrepreneur) Visa,' n.d.). Other applicants must have a minimum of £200,000 to invest in their business. Based on the above criteria, along with English language requirements, the minimum number of points earned must be 95, of which the majority (75 points) are allocated based on meeting investment criteria ('Tier 1 (Entrepreneur) Visa,' n.d.).

Tier 2 visa: This category encompasses 'skilled workers' in jobs on the Tier 2 Occupation list or Shortage Occupation list who have received a job offer in the UK or who are transferred to the UK by an international company, as well as skilled workers in areas for which there is a proven shortage in the UK, such as ministers of religion and sportspeople. Jobs on the tier 2 list must be offered to workers from within the Eurozone before those from outside are eligible. The perennial shortages plaguing the NHS has resulted in approximately 30% of Tier 2 visas being allocated to clinicians and ancillary staff; however, such shortages have recently been exacerbated by increasing limits placed on the numbers of these visas (Travis 2018)

Tier 3 visa: This category applies to low-skilled workers filling specific temporary labour shortages, such as the seasonal agricultural workers; however, since the institution of the five-tier system, the UK government has had a ready supply of such labourers from poorer countries in the Eurozone, and thus have never allocated any such visas.

Tier 4 visa: This category is for students aged over 16 interested in studying in the UK. Such individuals must already be accepted at a registered UK educational institution before they can apply.

Tier 5 visa: This category encompasses six sub-tiers of temporary, usually highly skilled workers who already have job offers and certificates of sponsorship from an established organisation, namely creative and sporting, charity, diplomatic or embassy workers, fellowships, religious workers, and the youth mobility scheme, which enables young people from countries that have reciprocal arrangements with the UK to work in the UK on working holidays.

Other UK Visas

Visitor visas, family visas, and some UK business visas are outside of the five tiers. UK visitor visas allow people to enter the country for short periods on business or pleasure, as well as short term business appointments, academic conferences, sporting events or creative/artistic work, and receiving private medical treatment ('UK Five Tier Points-Based Immigration System,' 2018). Family visas encompass those who wish to join a family member with British citizenship or those with permanent residency or indefinite leave to remain in the UK. There are also additional categories of family visas for the relatives of Eurozone nationals already living in the UK or are permanent UK residents or have the status of a 'qualified person'. Additionally, a limited number of UK business visas falling outside of the five-tier system permit senior employees to come to the country for the purpose of establishing the first UK branch or subsidiary of an overseas company ('UK Five Tier Points-Based Immigration System,' 2018). There is also a type of business visa available solely to Turkish nationals coming to the UK to set up a new business or to help run an existing enterprise ('UK Five Tier Points-Based Immigration System,' 2018).

'Overstayers' and Illegal Migration

Anyone with temporary leave to enter the UK who has remained in the country beyond the expiration of their visas is seen as an 'overstayer', which the UK Visas and Immigration agency (UKVI) defines as meaning that 'the applicant has overstayed their leave to enter/remain, not just stayed longer than they said they would'. The word 'illegal' is commonly used to describe people who entered Britain without visas; however, this term has been extended to encompass those who are now classified as overstayers, as such persons have breached the conditions of their visas. Other illegal migrants include those who entered the country by evading border patrols or using deceptive documents.

The Right to Refuse

From students to workers, many migrants from all over the world had previously used well-established routes to apply for a visa to enter the UK. However, since the changes initiated on July 9, 2012, rules have become much more restrictive.

Application approvals are subject to the discretion of the Home Office, and applications for entry can be refused for different reasons, such as when the applicant provides insufficient information on the form, or has omitted vital documents, such as a valid passport or identity card or a medical report. Other reasons could be that the application form was not completed correctly, or the information provided on the form was false, or counterfeit documents were submitted, even if the applicant is unaware of the deception (Home Office, 2018). If an applicant does not meet the established financial and 'good character' requirements, their application may be refused. The Home Office (2018) has published a comprehensive document spelling out its reasons for refusal of entry or leave to remain, among which some additional causes are stated below.

The Home Office will also refuse entry or leave to remain to individuals who have past criminal convictions. Unless the person can demonstrate refugee status, in cases when a person has previously served less than a year in prison, they cannot enter the country until five years have passed since the end of the sentence; if they have spent between one and four years in prison, they must wait 10 years. In some cases, even convictions not resulting in imprisonment may disqualify the applicant for entry, such as if the Secretary of State determined that the person's crime caused serious harm; or the individual is shown to be a persistent offender. Additionally, anyone owing the NHS over £500 or owing litigation costs to the Home Office may be refused entry (Home Office, 2018).

Anyone found to have previously violated UK immigration laws by 'overstaying', breaching conditions attached to his/her previous leave to remain, or entering illegally may be refused entry, unless the person only overstayed for 90 days or less and departed the country voluntarily and at his/her own expense. In cases of illegal or deceptive entry (Home Office 2018), the person must have entered over 10 years ago and the amount of time required since the person's departure varies based on whether they left voluntarily at their own expense (12 months), at the state's expense (two-five years depending on whether they left within six months of receiving notice), or was removed or deported (more than 10 years).

Other grounds may be more subjective. For example, a person may be refused entry simply because he/she has not satisfied the Immigration Officer that he/she is 'acceptable', or if the Immigration Officer determines that their exclusion is 'conducive to the public good' (Home Office, 2018). Reasons for such a determination may include past criminal activity not included in the above-stated criteria or may even be based on one's acquaintances and associates (Home Office, 2018).

Measures against Illegal Working, Money Accumulation and Renting

Since 1996, employers have been liable for financial penalties if they hire any person who is in breach of their conditions of stay in the United Kingdom, and powers have been given to employers to make periodic checks on employees who have limited leave to remain in the UK. However, the associated penalties clarify that most criminalisation related to immigration breaches remains attached to migrants, who can be imprisoned for up to six months and have their wages seized for working illegally (Home Office, 2016). Section 8 of the Asylum and Immigration Act 1996 threatened such employers with prosecutions; however, few of these actually occurred, and the Immigration and Asylum Act 2006 repealed the measure for most employers and replaced it with a regime of civil penalties, or fines, for employers of persons without leave or with leave with conditions which prevented them from working. Although the maximum fine is currently £20,000 per worker (Home Office, 2016) the government actually employs a sliding scale, which varies depending on upon the types of the eligibility checks undertaken, the number of occasions on which a warning or civil penalty has been incurred the degree of co-operation provided by the employer (Johnstone, 2017). Criminal penalties remain in force for businesses considered to be 'rogue' employers that knowingly hire ineligible migrants and convicted individuals can still receive prison sentences for up to five years (Home Office, 2016).

The hostile environment policy introduced through the Immigration Act 2014 initiated further limitations on overstayers, promoting immigration checks on driver's licence holders and revoking the licences of overstayers, obliging temporary migrants, including overseas students, to make a contribution to the NHS, as well as instituting a 'deport first, appeal later' policy for those who face no 'risk of serious irreversible harm' and severely reducing the grounds for appeal (Travis, 2013). Through the Immigration Act 2016, an amendment to the Immigration Act 2014 obliging banks to check the immigration status of all customers seeking to open new accounts, since January of 2018, banks and building societies have also been included in the requirement to check the immigration status of all current account holders against a government database of known illegal migrants, facing fines and public sanctions if they fail to conduct thorough immigration checks on current account holders (Treanor, 2017). Similarly, according to the Immigration Act 2014, 'right to rent' measures oblige private landlords and their agents to check the immigration status of residents and prospective tenants or risk a fine of up to £3,000 (Pickford, 2016). Landlords must not only review the original passports or other documents allowing tenants to live in the UK, they are also responsible for checking they are genuine and keeping copies (Pickford, 2016).

Justification for Tightening Controls: Cracking Down on Immigration Abuses

In justifying changes in regulations, the Home Office has often asserted that some immigrants have exploited certain loopholes in the system, and thus the new rules are meant to block these routes while also protecting 'legal' immigrants. We identify a few of these routes as follows:

Immigrants and the Welfare System

The welfare system is intended to be a means to an end or an aid for those who most need support. Refugees who are fleeing persecution and hunger should not be penalised for temporarily accessing these opportunities. However, the general perception about immigrants is that they come to the UK to live off of welfare, which does not take into the account that most people who came from non-EU countries are not allowed access to public funds. Fortunately for the children of these immigrants' schools do not yet fall under this category.

The experiences and expectations of immigrants vary depending on their country of origin. Although some immigrants—for example, new mothers or family with young children depending on it for livelihood—might use the welfare system for a short period upon their arrival to the UK, they soon seek to become financially independent, as their own pride will not allow them to continue to live on benefits. Moreover, it is not possible for most immigrants to survive and thrive on welfare benefits because the funds from this source are never enough. Some have responsibilities for other family members in their home countries that cannot be financed with the meagre income available to them through welfare. Unknown to much of the public, some immigrants combine work at two to three jobs so they can provide for their immediate and extended families and many even contribute to community projects in their home countries. Summarily, claims that all immigrants come to the UK because of welfare should henceforth be substantiated with facts, rather than surmises that only fuel anti-immigration sentiments.

Student Visa Route

It has been charged that some universities have admitted students who could not understand enough English to follow their courses, and some colleges and universities have been accused of collecting large sums of money from such students even while knowing that some of these might not be able to complete their programmes (Walls, 1999). Subsequently, these students enlist the services of English-speaking writers to write essays and sit exams for them. These students therefore end up graduating and entering the labour market without having attended the courses listed on their transcripts.

Students and colleges have also been accused of using the visa route as a means for students to illegally enter the UK labour market (Home Affairs Committee, 2009). Notwithstanding that they have paid the fees to the university and been allowed to enter the UK with student visas, once they have arrived in the country, they seek work within the labour market rather than pursuing the courses for which they were granted the visa. Others do enrol at the university; however, they spend far more hours working than attending school, or abandon the course halfway, thus defeating the purpose of the visa.

In some cases, unsuspecting students have been exploited by agents and ended up paying tuition fees, only to arrive in the UK and find out that such colleges were not registered with the home office or were not licensed to offer such courses. The exploitation of international students sometimes comes with assurances of being able to beat the law. According to a BBC report (Cook, 2015), one online advertisement assured students that 'if […] your college has lost the [visa-sponsoring] license, and you are not finding any option with reliable education provider in the UK to keep your status… If you want a student visa that allow [sic] you to work, please call us!'

Sham Marriages

Some immigrants have abused the marriage route as an opportunity to stay in the UK. The Home office defines a 'sham' marriage or civil partnership as 'a marriage or civil partnership entered for im-migration advantage by two people who are not a genuine couple' (Mowat, 2016). As opposed to a marriage or partnership entered into by a genuine couple for other reasons, including to ease immi-gration, sham marriage operates purely as a business, with no feel-ings of personal commitment. Both parties understand the deal, and it usually involves the migrant paying sums of money to gain access to legal settlement or other advantages, including access to other public services and benefits. People have been known to pay from as little as £250 to almost £30,000 for the marriage transac-tion, and the numbers of sham marriages—or at least suspicions of such—have dramatically increased to the point where over 7,600 suspicious weddings were reported to the Home Office over a peri-od of only two months in 2014 (Bennett, 2014).

Immigration Marriage Fraud

As opposed to a sham marriage, in which both partners are aware of the business nature of their agreement, marriage fraud occurs when a person living abroad or in the UK without a valid stay per-suades another into marrying them under false pretences of roman-ticism for the purposes of obtaining citizenship and financial gain from spouses and tax payers. Women are the most common victims of such scams; however, some men have also been so entrapped (Bennett, 2014). The unsuspecting victim genuinely assumes that the other party has romantic feelings for them, not realising that the other party's demonstrations of love were merely mechanisms to ensure their stay in the UK. Once their residency is confirmed, the 'husband' changes his behaviour and withdraws his claims of love, or simply absconds and deserts the marriage without notice, thus shattering the hopes and future of their victims.

Radicalisation and Extremism

As defined by the UK government, extremism includes the vocal or active opposition to such British values as democracy, the rule of law, individual liberty, mutual respect and tolerance of different faiths and beliefs, and in its most extreme manifestations, is expressed by support for terrorism and extremism, calling for the deaths of members of the armed forces, or active participation in terrorist activity (Home Office, 2011). A number of radicalised individuals have committed such acts after entering the UK on legal pretexts. According to official data, there were 54 deaths in Great Britain as a direct result of terrorist acts (excluding the perpetrators) for the period between from 11 September 2001 to 31 March 2016 (Allen & Dempsey, 2017). According to the director general of M15, whereas four terrorist attacks succeeded in killing 34 people, in 2017, nine additional attacks were prevented that year (Asthana, 2017).

The perpetrators of the terrorist attack in London on 7th July 2005 were found to be 'home-grown', having lived all or most of their lives in UK. In other cases, British nationals or citizens have journeyed to the Middle East to join terrorist groups such as ISIS/ISIL. Such cases are viewed as appalling aberrations, as they do not entail infiltration but rather constitute a betrayal of the country to which their families had fled for purposes of safety or economic opportunity. Many people asked why young men brought up in a 'system that had been so kind to them' would seek to destroy it. The government, and indeed, the entire nation has had to confront the fact that institutionalisation of the British identity is either not generally effective, or at the very least is having less than desired effects among some of its citizenry. Moreover, many of the very controls intended to prevent radicalism and extremism might end up fomenting such sentiments through the discrimination and hostility that so many ethnic minorities encounter in the UK, regardless of their country of birth.

Understanding the Barriers Experienced by the Black Minority Ethnic Groups

Ethnic minority individuals constitute a large and growing share of the UK population. Approximately one-third of ethnic minority individuals living in the UK were born in the country, whereas the remainder were born abroad.

There is no question but that immigration policies have a ripple effect on both documented and undocumented immigrants. It is difficult to obtain precise statistics of the immigrants that are being impacted by immigration restrictions; however, stressors are experienced by both illegal and legal migrants. Documented immigrants can be restricted from bringing over their dependants, and they might also be targeted by those in the community who hold racist views. Illegal immigrants may experience the frustration of not been able to work, the quagmire of waiting for decisions from the home office, and the fear of detention, deportation, and not knowing what awaits them should they be returned back to their country of origin.

Health problems. The human angle of immigration policies is hardly taken into consideration; however, dialogue with the African migrant groups suggests that uncertainty around their immigration status and the fear of been forcefully returned back to their countries has contributed to a deterioration in their physical health and mental health. Immigrants in this position have been known to experience failing physical health conditions such as high blood pressure, heart attacks and stroke. Others may suffer worsening mental health issues such as sleepless nights, post-traumatic stress disorder, anxiety, and psychosis, among others.

Language barriers. The integration of refugees from other countries includes their response to the English language. Language barriers continue to remain a difficulty for some of these refugees to rebuild their lives or reintegrate with their families following the compulsory language test before admission into the UK. The lack of provision of English classes remains a growing challenge in many councils, which further hinders community cohesion.

Inequality in education. Inequality in education is another growing challenge that impacts upon children from black minority ethnic families. Inequalities might be expressed through labelling of pupils and behaviour issues, grade predictions, negative peer pressure, and an ineffective support network for children of migrant parents.

Discrimination in the job market. Job discrimination may be evidenced in inequalities in hiring practises, whereby those with black/Asian sounding names receive fewer call backs after job interviews compared with candidates who have English names. Other areas of discrimination are visible in the number and extent of career opportunities that are available to those from the Black and other minority groups.

Recent Immigration Policies and the Windrush Generation

Although the UK government has listed a series of immigration abuses as justification for its increasingly xenophobic policies, anti-migrant measures have not been limited to those accused of committing the criminal acts described in the above section. Recently, the new rules have increasingly come to threaten the post-war generation of Caribbeans who came to the UK from the 1940s through the late 1960s. Most of these recruited workers carried British passports issued in the name of their islands, which were then British colonies; however, when those islands gained their independence, the workers were not told that they had effectively lost their citizenship would be required to obtain British naturalisation. Until the Immigration Act 1971, the only official record of the arrival of many Windrush immigrants were the landing cards collected as they disembarked from ships in UK ports, which were used by immigration officials for decades to verify their dates of arrival. However, in 2010 those landing cards were destroyed by the Home Office (Gentleman, 2018 30 June). Moreover, due to the fact that the Home Office did not keep a record of those granted leave to remain or issue any paperwork confirming their citizenship, many of these people and their Caribbean-born children have been unable to provide evidence of their national identity and therefore have been deemed illegal. Thus, although the Immigration Act 1971 gave people who had already settled in Britain indefinite leave to remain, many lack the documents to prove that they arrived before that date.

The introduction of the 'hostile environment' policy with the Immigration Act 2014 resulted in many members of the Windrush generation losing their jobs after routine citizenship checks, being unable to obtain unemployment benefits, and ultimately being driven to homelessness due to ineligibility even for emergency housing (Gentleman, 2018 21 February). Some have even been detained or deported in their old age, and many have been denied access to health services (Gentleman, 2017). After over half a century working and paying taxes in the UK, a number have determined to live underground amid constant fear and insecurity to reduce the risk of detention or deportation (Gentleman, 2018 21 February). Pressures have eased on these individuals after a national outcry following their publicisation, which resulted in a temporary halt to the hostile environment policy being placed in July 2018 (Bulman, 2018); however, many remain traumatised by their experiences and a number have yet to recover all that was taken from them. As of July of 2018, only 584 of the 2125 people who had contacted a 'Windrush hotline' had been granted citizenship, and the government had only been in contact with 14 of the dozens who were wrongfully deported (Bulman, 2018). As of August of 2018, numerous members of the Windrush generation were still living in homelessness and destitution and remain unable to access even basic services as they await a review of their cases by the Home Office (Marsh, 2018).

Conclusion

This chapter has examined the history of UK nationalisation and immigration policies and the routes by which people have historically arrived in the UK. It also documented the new immigration policies and presents case studies depicting their impact on different individual immigrants.

Throughout the 20th century, immigration and nationality law concepts engaged in an awkward mutual interaction in the aim of controlling immigration, and there was little attempt to tidy up the laws of nationality. Rather much of the new legislation was geared to stringently controlling both immigrants without and immigrants within the United Kingdom. Although the British Nationality Act 1981 thoroughly overhauled British nationality law, there is little doubt that it was as much an immigration Act as a nationality law, and the overriding considerations in its enactment related to immigration control (Juss, 1994). Unfortunately, such measures have not furthered the process of concretising nationality, and rather have resulted in alienating those who have already settled here. Despite a century's experience of modern immigration control and more than 30 years' experience of post-war colonial immigration, successive governments have shown themselves to be inept in the handling of these issues and have remained more concerned with the numbers of non-Whites accumulating in the country without considering the economic benefits of migrants (Juss, 1994). As we can see, the government has taken seriously the need for Britain to review its concept of citizenship in the light of political social and economic demands and the problems posed by globalisation. Becoming a British citizen has become a lengthy and bureaucratic process, and issues of immigration, nationality and freedom of movement have raised questions of the intersection between basic individual rights and the national interest (Noor, 2007). Anyone who overstays their visa in the UK—no matter how compelling the reason—is said to have committed a criminal offence. Although it is the prerogative of the state to protect its citizens, the wellbeing of immigrants is usually not taken into consideration when these policies are being made. One can only appreciate what could be going on in the mind of someone who has spent years or even decades in the UK, working hard and paying taxes; however, suddenly due to new changes in immigration rules, he or she becomes an overstayer due to an inability to switch to a category that would enable him or her to stay in the UK.

All too often, the laws of nationality have been reviewed with the aim to control Black and Asian immigration or a knee-jerk approach to a societal problem attributed to migrants because there is a general belief that political, economic, cultural and social problems are caused by migrants, particularly those from outside of Europe. The recent scandal affecting the Windrush migrants clarified for many that the primary aim of immigration policies has not been to curb illegal immigration, but rather to reduce and control the growth of Black and other ethnic minority communities. There is still much to be done concerning British immigration laws, which appear to be increasingly racially discriminatory in their aims and effect. Just as the patriality rule of 1971 barred Black and Asian migrants while maintaining the country's openness to Canadians and Australians, modern laws have tended to favour those from within the EU while becoming more and more restrictive to those from outside of the continent. Migrants from outside the EU are disproportionally channelled into lower paid jobs (Erel, Murji, & Nahaboo, 2016). For example, a study of Ghanaian migrants in London demonstrated how labour discrimination is reinforced by immigration status, whereby higher status positions are allocated first to EU migrants, while those holding temporary residence and restrictions on work (e.g. student visas) have found it increasingly difficult to access skilled jobs (Herbert, May, Wills, Datta, Evans, & McIlwaine, 2008). Most discussions of citizenship have considered the challenges posed by Britain's changing ethnic population. It is often said that people carry their ethics and values with them when they move into a new country, and there have been claims that the 'very glue' of British society is being weakened under the impact of rapidly growing communities of very diverse cultures—some of who are perceived as having no intention of integrating into UK life ('Immigration Truth that Labour Dare Not Speak,' 2007). Yet, many of these people come from countries that were historically exploited by Britain and incorporated into its Empire and have become gradually alienated from the rights this status has conferred on their White counterparts. For a nation that lays claim to celebrating the cultures of diverse people, the UK must develop better ways of concretising the British nationality.

The enormous outcry against international immigration has caused the government's focus to be directed toward reducing the numbers. Anti-immigrant sentiments create an atmosphere of xenophobia, which hinders community cohesion. However, it should not be obscured that many are contributing to the UK economically, socially, and in the area of politics. It is important to have an ongoing engagement with these communities in order to understand who they are and what their contributions are and have been. I hope to elaborate on this subject in subsequent volumes.

References

Allen, G., & Dempsey, N. (2017, 06 October). Terrorism in Great Britain: the statistics. Briefing paper number CBP7613. UK Office for National Statistics. Retrieved from researchbriefings.files.parliament.uk/documents/CBP-7613/CBP-7613.pdf

Asthana, A. (2017, 05 December). Nine terrorist attacks prevented in UK in last year, says MI5 boss. *The Guardian*. Retrieved from https://www.theguardian.com/uk-news/2017/dec/05/nine-terrorist-attacks-prevented-in-uk-in-last-year-says-mi5-boss

Barr, N. (2016, 22 July). Letter to friends (2): why Britain voted to leave, and what to do about it. London School of Economics. Retrieved from http://eprints.lse.ac.uk/73013/1/blogs.lse.ac.uk-Letter%20to%20friends%202%20why%20Britain%20voted%20to%20leave%20and%20what%20to%20do%20about%20it.pdf

Bennett, O. (2014, 19 February). Sham marriages occurring at a rate of one every hour, Government figures reveal. *Express.co.uk*. Retrieved from https://www.express.co.uk/news/uk/460639/Sham-marriages-occurring-at-a-rate-of-one-every-hour-Government-figures-reveal

Blinder, S. (2017, October 26). Migration to the UK: Asylum. The Migration Observatory, at the University of Oxford COMPAS (Centre on Migration, Policy and Society). Retrieved from http://www.migrationobservatory.ox.ac.uk/resources/briefings/migration-to-the-uk-asylum/

'British citizenship test tightened to include English test.' (2013, 17 April). *BBC News*. Retrieved from http://www.bbc.com/news/uk-politics-22158482

Bulman, M. (2018 12 July). Government halts 'hostile environment' immigration policy after Windrush scandal. *The Independent.* Retrieved from https://www.independent.co.uk/news/uk/home-news/hostile-environment-home-office-windrush-scandal-halt-sajid-javid-a8443486.html

'Citizenship points plan launched.' (2009, 03 August). *BBC News.* Retrieved fromhttp://news.bbc.co.uk/2/hi/8180749.stm

Cobain, I. (2011, 15 August). Home Office stripping more dual-nationality Britons of citizenship. *The Guardian*, Retrieved fromhttps://www.theguardian.com/uk/2011/aug/15/home-office-law-dual-citizenship

Cook, C. (2015, 16 July). Home Secretary proposes tougher rules for student visas. *BBC News.* Retrieved from http://www.bbc.com/news/uk-politics-33561040

Czaika, M., & de Haas, N. (2011, April). The effectiveness of immigration policies: A conceptual review of empirical evidence. IMI Working Paper Series, 33 International Migration Institute, University of Oxford. Retrieved from https://heindehaas.files.wordpress.com/2015/05/czaika-and-de-haas-2011-imi-wp33-the-effectiveness-of-immigration-policies-a-conceptual-review-of-empirical-evidence.pdf

Dent, E. (2018 05 July). Nye Bevan: the founding father of the NHS. *Healthcare Leader.* Retrieved from http://www.healthcareleadernews.com/nye-bevan-the-founding-father-of-the-nhs/

Dummett, A., & Nicol, A.G.L. (1990). *Subjects, Citizens, Aliens and Others: Nationality and Immigration Law.* Law in Context. London: Weidenfeld and Nicolson

Erel, U., Murji, K., & Nahaboo, Z. (2016) Understanding the contemporary race–migration nexus. *Ethnic and Racial Studies*, 39(8), 1339-1360.

Ford, S. (2018 20 April). NHS to establish nursing 'earn, learn and return' partnership with Caribbean country. *Nursing Times*. Retrieved from https://www.nursingtimes.net/news/workforce/ uk-government-does-deal-with-jamaica-to-recruit-nurses-for-nhs/7024177.article

Garuda Publications (2017, 05 March). Life in the UK test pass rates. Retrieved from http://www.garudapublications.com/wp-content/uploads/2017/03/Life-in-the-UK-Test-Pass-Rates-2017.pdf

Gentleman, A. (2017 28 November). 'I can't eat or sleep': the woman threatened with deportation after 50 years in Britain. *The Guardian*. Retrieved from https://www.theguardian.com/uk-news/2017/nov/28/i-cant-eat-or-sleep-the-grandmother-threatened-with-deportation-after-50-years-in-britain

Gentleman, A. (2018 21 February). 'I've been here for 50 years': the scandal of the former Commonwealth citizens threatened with deportation. *The Guardian*. Retrieved from https://www.theguardian.com/uk-news/2018/feb/21/ive-been-here-for-50-years-the-scandal-of-the-former-commonwealth-citizens-threatened-with-deportation

Gentleman, A. (2018 30 June). Home Office destroyed Windrush landing cards, says ex-staffer. *The Guardian*. Retrieved from https://www.theguardian.com/uk-news/2018/apr/17/home-office-destroyed-windrush-landing-cards-says-ex-staffer

Hasan, M. (2012, 04 July). Testing makes a mockery of Britishness. *New Statesman*. Retrieved from https://www.newstatesman.com/blogs/politics/2012/07/testing-makes-mockery-britishness

Herbert, J., May, J., Wills, J. Datta, K., Evans, Y., & McIlwaine, C. (2008). Multicultural Living? Experiences of Everyday Racism among Ghanaian Migrants in London. *European Urban and Regional Studies*, 15 (2), 103–117.

Home Affairs Committee (2009). Bogus colleges: eleventh report of session 2008-09.

Home Office. (1995) Immigration and Nationality Department Annual Report. London, UK: Home Office.

Home Office. (1998, 27 July). Fairer, Faster and Firmer -A Modern Approach to Immigration and Asylum. London, UK: Home Office.

Home Office. (2011, June). *Prevent* Strategy. London, UK: Home Office. Retrieved from https://www.gov.uk/government/uploads/system/uploads/attachment_data/file/97976/prevent-strategy-review.pdf

Home Office (2012, 12 June). Impact Assessment: Changes to Family Migration Rules. London, UK: Home Office. Retrieved from https://assets.publishing.service.gov.uk/government/uploads/system/uploads/attachment_data/file/257357/fam-impact-state.pdf

Home Office (2014, 11 March). Knowledge of language and life in the UK test results, 2009 to 2014. Retrieved from https://www.gov.uk/government/uploads/system/uploads/attachment_data/file/308769/FOI_30799_Statistics.pdf

Home Office (2016, July). Immigration Act 2016: factsheet – illegal working (Sections 34 -38). Retrieved from https://www.gov.uk/government/uploads/system/uploads/attachment_data/file/537205/Immigration_Act_-_Part_1_-_Illegal_Working.pdf

Home Office. (2018, 11 January). General grounds for refusal. Retrieved from https://www.gov.uk/government/uploads/system/uploads/attachment_data/file/673998/GGFR-Section-1-v29.0-EXT.PDF

'Immigration and Asylum Act 1999.' (2009, 19 January). The Guardian. Retrieved from https://www.theguardian.com/commentisfree/libertycentral/2009/jan/13/immigration-asylum-act

'Immigration Truth That Labour Dare Not Speak.' (2007, 24 October). The Telegraph. Retrieved from https://www.telegraph.co.uk/comment/3643526/Immigration-truth-that-Labour-dare-not-speak.html

Johnstone, J. (2017, 16 May). Why you might not have to pay a fine for illegal workers. Davidson Morris. Retrieved from https://www.davidsonmorris.com/fine-for-illegal-workers/

Joint Council for the Welfare of Immigrants. (2016, 27 January). Over half of British women would be blocked from bringing non-EEA spouse/ partner to UK under Immigration Rules. Retrieved from https://www.jcwi.org.uk/blog/2016/01/27/over-half-british-women-would-be-blocked-bringing-non-eea-spouse-partner-uk-under

Juss, S.S. (1994). Immigration, Nationality, and Citizenship. Citizenship and the Law Series. London, UK: Bloomsbury Publishing PLC.

Karatani, R. (2003). Defining British Citizenship: Empire, Commonwealth and Modern Britain. (British Politics and Society). London, UK: Frank Cass

Kemp, P. (2008, 04 April). School 'helps citizenship cheats'. BBC News. Retrieved from http://news.bbc.co.uk/2/hi/uk_news/politics/7330338.stm

Kemp, P. (2008, 05 April). How UK citizenship tests are 'abused'. *BBC News*. Retrieved from http://news.bbc.co.uk/2/hi/uk_news/politics/7331550.stm

Marsh, S. (2018 10 August). Windrush citizens still waiting for cases to be resolved. *The Guardian*. Retrieved from https://www.theguardian.com/uk-news/2018/aug/10/windrush-citizens-still-waiting-for-cases-to-be-resolved

'Men jailed for UK citizenship fraud in Sheffield.' (2010, 24 February). *BBC News*. Retrieved from http://news.bbc.co.uk/2/hi/uk_news/england/south_yorkshire/8535341.stm

Mowat, L. (2016, 28 February). EXCLUSIVE: Sham marriages have increased by almost 850% and authorities 'are overwhelmed'. *Express.co.uk*. Retrieved at https://www.express.co.uk/news/uk/648025/Sham-marriages-increased-by-almost-850-and-authorities-are-overwhelmed-warns-MP

Noor, O. (2007). Review of Life in the UK. Journal of Immigration Asylum and Nationality Law, 12(2), 166-168.

Parry, C. (1957). *Nationality and Citizenship Laws of the Commonwealth and of the Republic of Ireland*. Vol.1. London, UK: Stevens.

Pickford, J. (2016, 31 January). UK landlords must check tenants' immigration status or face fine. *Financial Times*. Retrieved from https://www.ft.com/content/d5c52c16-c5de-11e5-b3b1-7b2481276e45

Seddon, D. (Ed.) Immigration, Nationality and Refugee Law Handbook. London, UK: Joint Council for the Welfare of Immigrants.

Snow, S. & Jones, E. (2011 08 March). Immigration and the National Health Service: putting history to the forefront. *History & Policy*, Policy Papers. Retrieved from http://www.historyandpolicy.org/

policy-papers/papers/immigration-and-the-national-health-service-putting-history-to-the-forefron

Spencer, S. (1994). *Strangers & Citizens: a positive approach to migrants and refugees.* London, UK: IPPR/Rivers Oram Press.

Spencer, S. (1998). The impact of immigration policy on race relations. In T. Blackstone, B. Parekh and P. Sanders (Eds). *Race Relations in Britain* (pp. 74-95). London, UK: Routledge.

'Test faker conman is jailed.' (2011, 01 March). *Lancashire Post.* Retrieved from https://www.lep.co.uk/news/crime/test-faker-conman-is-jailed-1-3129033

Travis, A. (2013 10 October). Immigration bill: Theresa May defends plans to create 'hostile environment'. *The Guardian.* Retrieved from https://www.theguardian.com/politics/2013/oct/10/immigration-bill-theresa-may-hostile-environment

Travis, A. (2018 18 February). NHS and other key employers face staffing crisis as Home Office refuses visa applications. *The Guardian.* Retrieved from https://www.theguardian.com/uk-news/2018/feb/18/uk-hits-skilled-worker-visa-cap-third-month-home-office-refuses-applications

Treanor, J. (2017, 18 December). UK banks face fines as immigration checks on account holders loom. *The Guardian.* Retrieved from https://www.theguardian.com/business/2017/dec/18/uk-banks-face-fines-as-immigration-checks-on-account-holders-loom

'UK Borders Act 2007.' (2009, 19 January). *The Guardian.* Retrieved from https://www.theguardian.com/commentisfree/libertycentral/2008/dec/16/uk-borders-act

Walls, R. (1999, 02 December). Education: The Recruitment Scandal: UK universities are `exploiting' foreign students. *The Independent.* *Retrieved from* https://www.independent.co.uk/news/education/education-news/education-the-recruitment-scandal-uk-universities-are-exploiting-foreign-students-1125149.html